Cupcakes
from the Primrose Bakery

Cupcakes
from the Primrose Bakery

Martha Swift
&
Lisa Thomas

Photography by Yuki Sugiura

Kyle Cathie Limited

For Daisy and Millie, Thomas and Ned

First published in Great Britain in 2009 by
Kyle Cathie Limited
23 Howland Street
London W1T 4AY
www.kylecathie.com

ISBN 978 1 85626 847 9

10 9

Photographer Yuki Sugiura *
Illustrations Michael Heath
Designer Nicky Collings
Props Stylist Cynthia Inions
Food Stylist Linda Tubby
Project Editor Sophie Allen
Copy Editor Stephanie Evans
Proofreader Ruth Baldwin
Production Gemma John

* except for author photograph on page 8: Elizabeth Scheder-Bieschin

A Cataloguing in Publication record for this title is available from the
British Library.

Colour reproduction by Colourscan
Printed in China by C&C Offset Printing Co., Ltd.

Contents

Introduction

In October 2004 we started baking cupcakes for children's parties in Primrose Hill, North London. We were two mothers, each with two young children. We had discovered that the kind of cakes we had in mind – tasting as delicious as they looked and looking as good as they tasted – were not to be found. It also quickly became clear to us that the cakes we made were being eaten as much by the adults as by the children. We knew that cupcakes were very popular in Australia and America: why not in the UK? Their simplicity and versatility make them perfect for almost every occasion or just everyday. You can make as many or as few as you need and decorate them extravagantly or totally simply. Most people, of every age, sex and background seem to enjoy eating them!

Our idea was very simple. We wanted to produce cupcakes from natural ingredients, using no preservatives and no artificial colours, ingredients or flavours. And, equally important, we wanted them to look amazing and totally distinctive. To do this, we knew we had to find the decorations outside the UK. We went to the US, to Italy, to Australia and to the Philippines in search of original and appealing sugar cake decorations – flowers, sprinkles, animals, butterflies. This has since grown to take in decorations for every possible occasion and public holiday – from Valentine's Day to Halloween, from Mothers' Day to Christmas Day.

Our first cakes were baked at home, in a domestic oven in Lisa's kitchen (which was always full of children) in between the school run and the ironing. Soon after selling our cupcakes to a local delicatessen, Melrose and Morgan in Primrose Hill, on a daily basis, we were approached by Selfridges Food Hall. We became their first supplier of cupcakes and their first supplier from a domestic kitchen. Since then we have expanded to sell to Fortnum and Mason, Liberty, and other major food stores. Because our cupcakes are all made with natural ingredients we were also able to start supplying Fresh and Wild.

Very early on we began to get orders for private functions. At first, these mainly took the shape of children's parties, christenings and birthdays. But quickly we were asked to provide cupcakes for every other kind of event, both private and public. We have done book launches with themes, such as all-orange mini cupcakes for the Orange Prize for Fiction. We have supplied cakes for designers for

introduction

Fashion Week. We have made cupcakes for Elton John's 60th birthday party and for the Brits music awards. We are lucky enough to work on a regular basis with outstanding British fashion brands such as Anya Hindmarch, LK Bennett, Miller Harris, Topshop and Paul Smith. Each time the cakes are tailored to the occasion and the demands of our customers. And we have developed an alternative to the traditional wedding cake, in the form of pyramids of cupcakes, iced and decorated with flowers, both sugar and fresh. We now cater to occasions all over southern England.

In the autumn of 2006 we realised that we had outgrown Lisa's kitchen. We opened our first bakery and cafe in Primrose Hill, baking everything on site. We wanted to create an environment to go with the cupcakes – customers can come for freshly baked croissants, cakes and biscuits while having excellent coffee and tea. The smells rising from the kitchen below bring in people from the whole neighbourhood. We have kept to our original idea: everything is baked and iced by hand and every cupcake is individual. In November 2008 we opened our second shop in Tavistock Street in Covent Garden, run along the same principles as our first shop, with all the cakes and other pastries baked in the basement and a small cafe on the ground floor so that customers may eat in or take away.

Nearly five years on, we are still determined to hold on to our idea of a home-baking, less industrial type of bakery. Our recipes are straightforward and can be made in ordinary kitchens with no special equipment or skills. In this book we show how easy it is to produce – in a world increasingly given over to production lines and fancy packaging – a cake that is delicious, pretty and without artificial ingredients. We always recommend using seasonal and well sourced ingredients as it makes such a difference to the finished product.

It is not simply about cupcakes. It is about producing food that is different – that looks different and tastes different. It is about food that smells delicious and that you want to eat. Cupcakes suit any and every occasion and every imaginable person, from a five-year-old to a bride, from proud new parents to celebrating octogenarians. We want to demonstrate how, if you believe in these ideas, if you follow these simple recipes, it can be both pleasurable and rewarding.

Basic Cupcakes

Much of the appeal of cupcakes lies in the relative ease with which they can be prepared and their versatility. Four basic cupcake sponge recipes – vanilla, chocolate, lemon and carrot – can be made in any quantity, iced with a variety of buttercreams and dressed up or down, as the occasion demands. These basics are a great place to start if you are new to baking or to which you can return time and time again, however experienced a baker you are.

To guarantee a perfect cupcake sponge, these are the golden rules we always follow: First, always use good-quality ingredients and bring everything to room temperature before you start to mix them. Try also to be very precise with weighing or measuring. It's well worth investing in a set of electronic scales for accurate amounts: some weigh in millilitres as well as grams so you can use them for liquid as well as dry weights. Always sift flour and baking powder to avoid lumps. We advise you to use an electric hand mixer if possible, as they make it so much quicker and easier to beat the ingredients together and to get a good consistency, but obviously you can beat the mixtures by hand, if you wish. And, to ensure all those carefully measured ingredients end up as cake, use a rubber spatula to scrape down the sides of the bowl to ensure the batter mixture is well combined. Next, it's just as important to be accurate with the oven temperatures and cooking times and – as with pretty much all baking – don't be tempted to open the oven door while the cupcakes are cooking as even a small amount of cold air tends to make the sponge sink. Lastly, when you turn out your cupcakes, do allow them to cool completely before icing and, if possible, ice and eat them on the same day, when the sponge is at its freshest. Alternatively the cupcakes can be stored in airtight containers before you ice them. They will keep for up to three days at room temperature. Do not refrigerate.

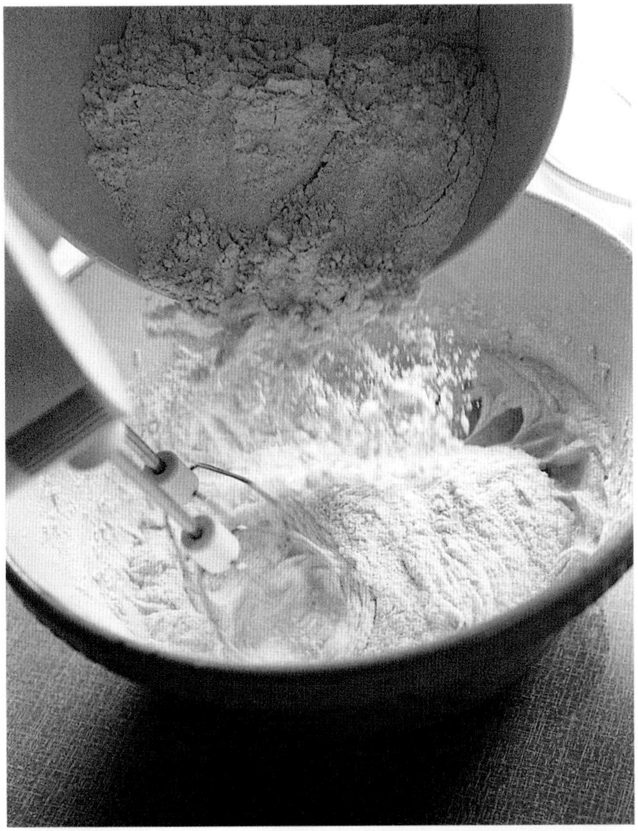
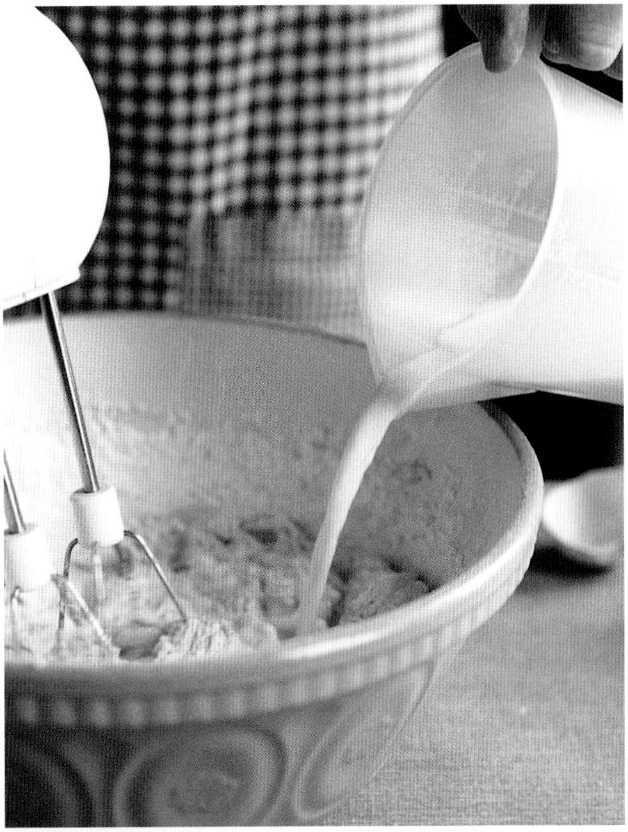
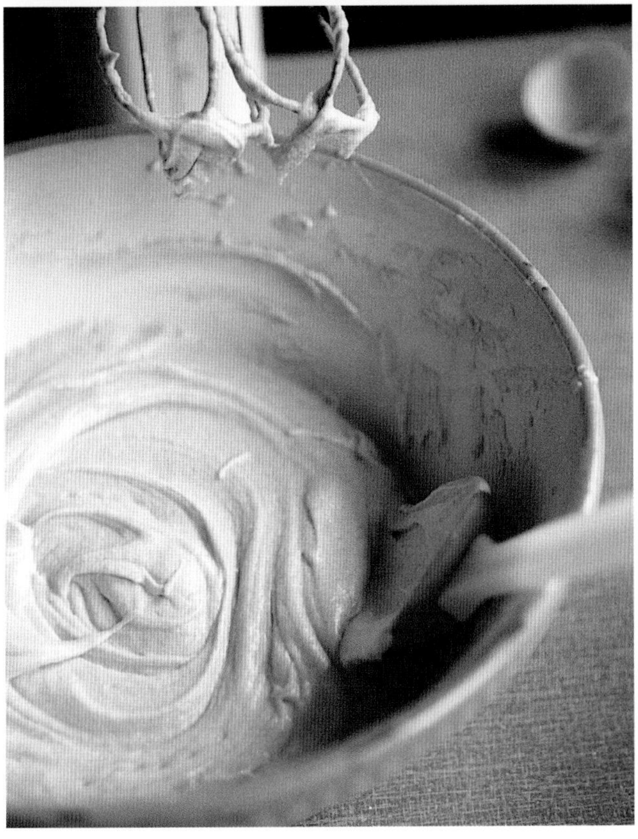
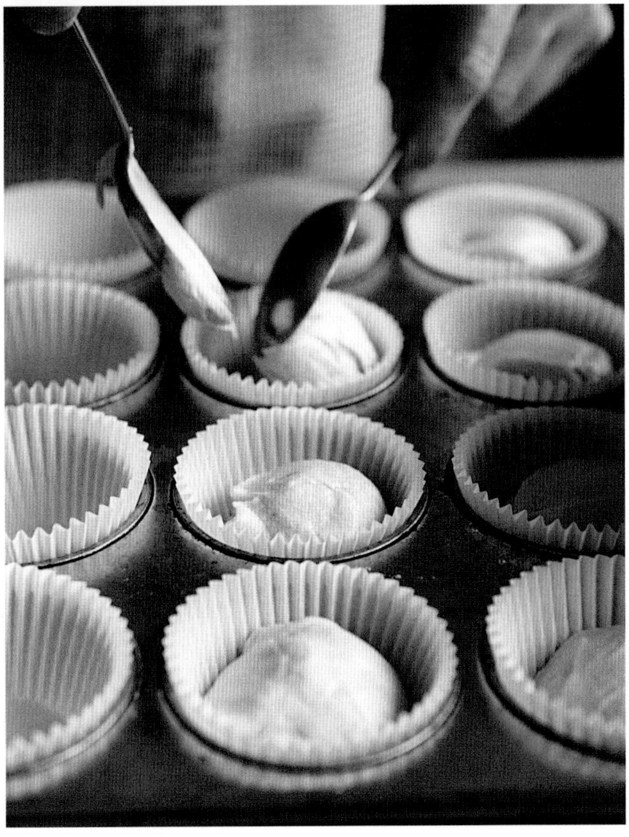

Vanilla Cupcakes

This is our classic cupcake; it takes a lead role in our kitchens with its huge versatility as it can be dressed in a variety of icings and adorned with decorations that will take it from one occasion to another.

Preheat the oven to 160°C (fan)/180°C/350°F/gas mark 4 and line a 12-hole muffin tray or three 12-hole mini muffin trays with the appropriate size cupcake cases.

In a large mixing bowl cream the butter and sugar until the mixture is pale and smooth, which should take 3–5 minutes using an electric hand mixer. Add the eggs, one at a time, mixing for a few minutes after each addition.

Combine the two flours in a separate bowl. Put the milk in a jug and add the vanilla extract to it.

Add one-third of the flours to the creamed mixture and beat well. Pour in one-third of the milk and beat again. Repeat these steps until all the flour and milk have been added.

Carefully spoon the mixture into the cupcake cases, filling them to about two-thirds full. Bake in the oven for about 25 minutes (regular size) or 15 minutes (mini size) until slightly raised and golden brown. To check they are cooked, insert a skewer in the centre of one of the cakes – it should come out clean.

Remove from the oven and leave the cakes in their tins for about 10 minutes before carefully placing on a wire rack to cool. Once they are completely cool, ice the cupcakes with vanilla, chocolate, or lime and coconut buttercream icing.

Makes 12 regular or
36 mini cupcakes

110g unsalted butter, at room
   temperature
225g caster sugar, preferably
   golden
2 large eggs, free-range or organic
150g self-raising flour, sifted
125g plain flour, sifted
120ml semi-skimmed milk, at
   room temperature
1 teaspoon good-quality
   vanilla extract

Chocolate Cupcakes

Always a favourite, these moist chocolate cupcakes are great, made regular size or as minis. They can be used with a number of our buttercreams, making them all the more delicious!

Makes 16 regular or 48 mini cupcakes

115g good-quality dark chocolate (70% cocoa solids)
85g unsalted butter, at room temperature
175g soft brown sugar
2 large eggs, free-range or organic, separated
185g plain flour, sifted
¾ teaspoon baking powder
¾ teaspoon bicarbonate of soda
Pinch of salt
250ml semi-skimmed milk, at room temperature
1 teaspoon good-quality vanilla extract

Preheat the oven to 170°C (fan)/190°C/375°F/gas mark 5 and line a couple of 12-hole muffin trays or four 12-hole mini muffin trays with the appropriate size cupcake cases.

Break the chocolate into pieces and melt. The easiest way is to put it in a plastic bowl or jug in a microwave on a medium heat for 30 seconds, stir and then microwave again for a further 30 seconds – but be very careful not to burn the chocolate. Alternatively, put the pieces in a heatproof bowl over a saucepan of barely simmering water. Stir occasionally until it has completely melted and is quite smooth. Leave to cool slightly.

In a large bowl cream the butter and sugar until the mixture is pale and smooth, which should take 3–5 minutes using an electric hand mixer. In a separate bowl and with clean beaters, beat the egg yolks for several minutes. Slowly add the egg yolks to the creamed mixture and beat well. Next, add the melted chocolate to the mixture and beat well.

Combine the flour, baking powder, bicarbonate of soda and salt in a separate bowl. Put the milk in a jug and add the vanilla extract to it. Add one-third of the flour to the chocolate mixture and beat well. Pour in one-third of the milk and beat again. Repeat these steps until all the flour and milk have been added. In a clean bowl, whisk the egg whites until soft peaks start to form. Carefully fold the egg whites into the batter, using a metal spoon. Do not beat or you will take all the air out of the mixture.

Carefully spoon the mixture into the cupcake cases, filling them to about two-thirds full. This is a fairly liquid batter, so take care when spooning out as it can end up being very messy! Alternatively, pour the batter into the cases from a jug to make it easier. Bake in the oven for 20–25 minutes (regular size) or 15 minutes (mini size). To check they are cooked, insert a skewer in the centre of one of the cakes – it should come out clean. Remove from the oven and leave the cakes in their tins for about 10 minutes before carefully placing on a wire rack to cool. Once they are completely cool, ice the cupcakes with chocolate, vanilla or coffee buttercream.

These cupcakes can be stored at room temperature for 3 days in an airtight container before icing. They are very moist, so they keep very well if stored correctly.

Lemon Cupcakes

These fresh lemon cupcakes are always very popular in our bakery and also at weddings and christenings. Make sure you use really plump juicy lemons for maximum zing!

Preheat the oven to 160°C (fan)/180°C/350°F/gas mark 4 and line a 12-hole muffin tray with the appropriate size cupcake cases.

In a large mixing bowl cream the butter and sugar until the mixture is pale and smooth, which should take 3–5 minutes using an electric hand mixer. Add the eggs, one at a time, mixing for a few minutes after each addition.

Combine the two flours in a separate bowl and combine the milk, lemon juice and sour cream in a jug. Add one-third of the flours to the creamed mixture and beat well. Pour in one-third of the milk and beat again. Repeat these steps until all the flour and milk have been added, incorporating the lemon zest with the last third of flour. Don't worry if the mixture starts to curdle: simply add another spoonful of plain flour and beat well.

Carefully spoon the mixture into the cupcake cases, filling them to about two-thirds full. Bake in the oven for about 25 minutes until slightly raised and golden brown. To check they are cooked, insert a skewer in the centre of one of the cakes – it should come out clean.

Remove from the oven and leave the cakes in their tins for about 10 minutes before carefully placing on a wire rack to cool. Once they are completely cool, you can ice the cupcakes with lemon buttercream (see page 31) and decorate with a sugared lemon slice (you'll find pots of these in the baking aisle of most supermarkets) or a little finely grated lemon zest.

Makes 12 regular cupcakes

110g unsalted butter, at room temperature
225g caster sugar, preferably golden
2 large eggs, free-range or organic
150g self-raising flour, sifted
125g plain flour, sifted
90ml semi-skimmed milk, at room temperature
2 tablespoons freshly squeezed lemon juice
1 tablespoon sour cream
Grated zest of 1 lemon (you need 1 teaspoon)

Carrot Cupcakes

With all those carrots and raisins, these moist little cakes feel like they must be good for you! They can be eaten warm as a great start to your morning or topped with our orange cream cheese icing (see page 35). They are also perfect for a less sweet afternoon treat.

Preheat the oven to 160°C (fan)/180°C/350°F/gas mark 4 and line a couple of 12-hole muffin trays with the appropriate size and number of cupcake cases.

Finely grate the carrots and drain off any liquid. Combine the grated carrots and raisins in a large bowl using a wooden spoon and put to one side.

In a large mixing bowl beat the eggs and sugar together for several minutes and then add the oil, vanilla extract and orange zest and beat well.

Sift the flour, bicarbonate of soda, salt and cinnamon into a separate bowl, then gradually add these ingredients to the egg and sugar mixture, beating well after each addition. Pour this mixture into the bowl containing the carrots and raisins and incorporate using a wooden spoon or spatula until they are evenly blended.

Carefully spoon the mixture into the cupcake cases, filling them to about two-thirds full. Bake in the oven for about 25 minutes – the cupcakes will be quite dark brown in colour and feel 'spongy' to the touch. Remove from the oven and leave the cakes in their tins for about 10 minutes before carefully placing on a wire rack to cool.

These cupcakes often look a bit smaller than some of the other recipes and are a much moister sponge. If you are icing them with orange cream cheese icing, it's nice to finish them off with a sprinkling of cinnamon.

Makes about
15 regular cupcakes

225g carrots, peeled and trimmed
130g raisins
2 large eggs, free-range or organic
130g caster sugar, preferably
  golden
120ml corn oil
½ teaspoon good-quality
  vanilla extract
Grated zest of 1 orange (you
  need 2 teaspoons)
120g plain flour
1 teaspoon bicarbonate of soda
Pinch of salt
1 teaspoon ground cinnamon

Basic Icings

The secret to perfect buttercream icing is to beat the mixture for long enough (preferably with an electric hand mixer), which is always much longer than you might imagine! Aim to beat your icing for several minutes until it is very smooth and creamy. Sifting the icing sugar after you weigh it out also helps to ensure the ideal consistency.

The ingredients for these six basic buttercream icing recipes are simple and few, but by choosing high-quality vanilla extract, plain chocolate and espresso powder and selecting ripe and juicy citrus fruit, you will ensure that the end result will taste fantastic.

Buttercream icing should always be stored in airtight containers at room temperature and – apart from the cream cheese icing – never refrigerated. It keeps well for up to three days and so it can be used with one type of cupcake sponge one day and another the next. Simply beat the icing again with an electric hand mixer or a wooden spoon to get it to the right consistency before using.

How to ice a cupcake

Practice makes perfect with icing cupcakes! It is strangely much more difficult than it looks. We hope this step-by-step guide will help you achieve the perfect result.

1 To keep the consistency of the buttercream icing as smooth as possible, beat the icing with an electric hand beater before starting. Between icing each cupcake, use a knife to stir the icing.

2 Start by scooping up the most buttercream you can in one go with a palette knife and place it in the centre of the cupcake.

3 Keeping the knife angled so that its flat side remains in contact with the buttercream, work the icing out to one edge of the cupcake by gently pushing it using small strokes with the knife (see top left).

4 Take another scoop of buttercream icing and repeat step 3, this time pushing the icing out to the opposite edge of the cupcake (see top right).

5 Add one more scoop of icing to the cupcake to bring the edges together, whilst making a central peak with the remaining icing (see bottom left).

6 Dip the end of the knife into the centre of the iced cupcake and, in an anti-clockwise direction, drag the knife in a circular motion to create a swirl effect (see bottom right).

7 Decorate the cupcake as desired. Make sure to put any sprinkles on to the cupcakes as quickly as possible, otherwise the icing will set a little, making it hard for any decoration to stick.

step by step!

Vanilla Buttercream Icing

This is our favourite and most traditional icing recipe. Simple and unadorned, it lends itself perfectly to many of our cupcakes and layer cakes, but by all means tint it with a little colour if you wish. We can't stress too much how the flavour and consistency are dependent on the quality of these simple ingredients, so don't buy anything but the best.

In a large mixing bowl beat the butter, milk, vanilla extract and half the icing sugar until smooth – this can take several minutes with an electric hand mixer. Gradually add the remainder of the icing sugar and beat again until the buttercream is smooth and creamy.

If you want to colour your buttercream, always start with one drop of colouring and beat thoroughly. This will be all you need to achieve a very pale pastel hue. Add carefully, drop by drop, and beat after each addition to build up to your desired shade.

Makes enough to ice
15–20 regular or about
60 mini cupcakes

**110g unsalted butter, at room
   temperature**
**60ml semi-skimmed milk, at
   room temperature**
**1 teaspoon good-quality
   vanilla extract**
500g icing sugar, sifted
**Few drops of food colouring
   (optional)**

Chocolate Buttercream Icing

This makes a rich, velvety chocolate buttercream. It's irresistible; anything iced with this one is always quickly devoured by adults and children alike. Use generously on cupcakes and layer cakes for the ultimate chocolate treat.

Melt the chocolate in a bowl or plastic jug in the microwave until smooth and of a thick pouring consistency. A general guide would be to heat at 30-second intervals on medium, stirring in between, to avoid burning the chocolate. Alternatively melt the chocolate in a heatproof glass bowl over a saucepan of barely simmering water. Stir occasionally until it has completely melted and is quite smooth. Leave to cool slightly.

In a large mixing bowl beat the butter, milk, vanilla and icing sugar until smooth – this can take several minutes with an electric hand mixer. Add the melted chocolate and beat again until thick and creamy. If it looks too runny to use when trying to ice cupcakes or cakes, simply keep beating – this will thicken the icing and improve its consistency.

Makes enough to ice
15–20 regular or
60 mini cupcakes

175g good-quality dark chocolate (70% cocoa solids)
225g unsalted butter, at room temperature
1 tablespoon semi-skimmed milk, at room temperature
1 teaspoon good-quality vanilla extract
250g icing sugar, sifted

Lemon Buttercream Icing

This lemon buttercream perfectly complements our lemon cupcakes or layer cake – its citrus tang makes it the perfect foil for the sweet cake. It also smells delicious!

In a large mixing bowl beat the butter, lemon juice, lemon zest and half the icing sugar until smooth – this can take several minutes with an electric hand mixer. Gradually add the remainder of the icing sugar and beat again until smooth and creamy.

Use this icing on the lemon cupcakes (see page 19) or inside and on top of the lemon layer cake (see page 134).

Makes enough to ice
15–20 regular cupcakes or
1 'two-layer' cake

110g unsalted butter, at room temperature
2 tablespoons freshly squeezed lemon juice
Grated zest of 1–2 unwaxed lemons (you need 2 teaspoons)
500g icing sugar, sifted

Coffee Buttercream Icing

This is real coffee buttercream, with its full flavour coming from good espresso powder. Partnered with our chocolate sponge cupcakes (see page 16), it becomes a mocha hit.

150g unsalted butter, at room temperature
1 tablespoon semi-skimmed milk, at room temperature
2 teaspoons instant espresso powder, dissolved in a small amount of hot water
350g icing sugar, sifted

In a large mixing bowl beat the butter, milk, espresso mixture and half the icing sugar until smooth – this can take several minutes with an electric hand mixer. Gradually add the remainder of the icing sugar to produce a buttercream of a creamy and smooth consistency.

Orange Cream Cheese Icing

Less sweet, but no less delicious than our traditional buttercream icings, this fresh, creamy icing is the natural choice for the carrot cupcakes but it would be a great one for the marmalade cupcakes, too (see page 44).

Place all the ingredients in a mixing bowl and beat well until thoroughly combined and the icing is smooth and pale – this can take several minutes with an electric hand mixer.

Cream cheese icing must be stored in the fridge, but it keeps well. Before re-using, allow it come to room temperature and then beat again.

Makes enough to ice
15–20 regular or about
60 mini cupcakes

175g cream cheese
450g icing sugar, sifted
125g unsalted butter, at room
temperature
Grated zest of 1 orange

Lime and Coconut Buttercream

For a more exotic flavour, this combination of fresh lime and coconut always satisfies. Great on vanilla cupcakes, but how about trying it with the ginger cupcakes (see page 83)?

Makes enough to ice
15–20 regular or about
60 mini cupcakes

115g unsalted butter, at room temperature
2 tablespoons freshly squeezed lime juice
Grated zest of 1–2 limes (you need 2 teaspoons)
500g icing sugar, sifted
Handful of desiccated coconut, to decorate

In a large mixing bowl beat the butter, lime juice and zest and half the icing sugar until smooth – this can take several minutes with an electric hand mixer. Gradually add the remainder of the icing sugar and beat until thick and creamy.

Use this icing on vanilla cupcakes and finish with a sprinkling of coconut. The icing will set slightly if left, so make sure to put the coconut on at once.

tip

For a special occasion, you could even place fresh orchids on top of the cakes, as the beauty of these exotic flowers goes so well with these cupcakes.

Festive and Seasonal

On the following pages you'll find ideas for seasonal cupcakes and celebrations and special days throughout the year. Of course you don't have to reserve these cupcakes for the times and events of the year we have suggested, though some of the recipes are intended to celebrate fresh seasonal ingredients, such as strawberries in the summer months and cranberries around Christmas time. And by all means deviate from our suggested decorations for these cupcakes to suit your particular occasion. You don't have to decorate them at all; they'll still be a treat, any day of the week!

The preparation of some of these cupcakes and icings is a step beyond the basic recipes of the preceding chapters, but they can be made by almost anyone and enjoyed by all. Just don't forget the importance of good-quality ingredients, and patience.

Honey and Granola Cupcakes

As the New Year begins, it feels good to shake off a little of the over-indulgence of the holidays. It feels good too to produce something made in your own kitchen, especially using the wholesome ingredients that go into this recipe. Besides being an all-day energy-boosting treat, they are completely satisfying and delicious warmed for breakfast, simply served plain, spread with honey and butter, or topped with cream cheese icing.

Makes about
12 regular cupcakes

110g unsalted butter, at room
   temperature
120g light soft brown sugar
175g clear honey
2 large eggs, free-range or organic
220g plain flour, sifted
½ teaspoon bicarbonate of soda
½ teaspoon baking powder
½ teaspoon salt
65ml semi-skimmed milk, at
   room temperature
½ teaspoon good-quality
   vanilla extract
65ml low-fat plain yogurt
250g granola (pick out any large
   whole nuts if you can)

Preheat the oven to 160°C (fan)/180°C/350°F/gas mark 4 and line a 12-hole muffin tray with the appropriate size cupcake cases.

In a large mixing bowl cream the butter, sugar and honey until the mixture is light and fluffy, which should take about 2–3 minutes using an electric hand mixer. Add the eggs, one at a time, mixing for a few minutes after each addition.

Combine the plain flour, bicarbonate of soda, baking powder and salt in a separate bowl. Combine the milk, vanilla extract and yogurt in a jug. Add one-third of the flour mixture to the creamed mixture and beat well. Pour in one-third of the milk and yogurt and beat again. Repeat these steps until all the flour and milk have been added. Fold in the granola carefully to incorporate evenly.

Carefully spoon the mixture into the cupcake cases, filling them to about two-thirds full. Bake in the oven for about 25 minutes until golden brown. To check they are cooked, insert a skewer in the centre of one of the cakes – it should come out clean.

Remove from the oven and leave the cakes in their tins for about 10 minutes. Serve warm with butter and honey or with a little cream cheese icing (see page 35) made without the orange zest.

Blueberry and Polenta Cupcakes

Somewhere between a cupcake and a muffin, this recipe works perfectly for breakfast or makes a healthier snack during the day or at teatime. The use of polenta gives a satisfying crunchy texture, coupled with the delicious taste and colour of the blueberries.

Preheat the oven to 160°C (fan)/180°C/350°F/gas mark 4 and line one or two 12-hole muffin trays with the appropriate size and number of cupcake cases.

In a large mixing bowl cream the butter and sugars until pale and smooth, which should take 3–5 minutes using an electric hand mixer. Add the eggs, one at a time, mixing for a few minutes after each addition.

Combine the plain flour, polenta, bicarbonate of soda, baking powder and salt in a separate bowl. Add one-third of the flour mix to the creamed mixture and beat until just combined. Add half of the buttermilk and mix until just combined. Repeat these steps until all the flour mix and buttermilk have been added. Gently fold in the blueberries.

Carefully spoon the mixture into the cupcake cases, filling them to about two-thirds full. Bake in the oven for about 25 minutes until slightly raised and golden brown. To check they are cooked, insert a skewer in the centre of one of the cakes – it should come out clean.

Remove from the oven and leave the cakes in their tins for about 10 minutes. These are delicious served still warm, maybe with some butter and a few fresh blueberries. You could dust the tops of the cupcakes with a little icing sugar before serving.

Makes about
14 regular cupcakes

110g unsalted butter, at room
    temperature
110g demerara sugar
120g soft light brown sugar
2 large eggs, free-range or organic
160g plain flour, sifted
140g fine-ground polenta
½ teaspoon bicarbonate of soda
½ teaspoon baking powder
½ teaspoon salt
125ml buttermilk
130g blueberries, fresh or frozen,
    at room temperature
Icing sugar, for dusting (optional)

tip
To prevent the blueberries from sinking in the cupcakes, toss them gently in a little plain flour before folding them into the batter.

Frances' Pecan and Orange Marmalade Cupcakes

These delicious cupcakes were devised by one of our chefs, Frances Money, as a great breakfast food, particularly during the New Year winter months after Christmas, when we are all trying to be a bit more healthy after all the rich festive food. A great start to the day, especially served straight from the oven and maybe even with a bit more marmalade on the side!

Makes about
12 regular cupcakes

55g unsalted butter,
    melted and cooled
125ml corn oil
60ml orange juice (juice of
    approx. 1 small orange)
Grated zest of 1 small orange
80g thick-cut orange marmalade
¼ teaspoon good-quality
    vanilla extract
250g plain flour, sifted
1 teaspoon bicarbonate of soda
½ teaspoon salt
2 large eggs, free-range or organic
180g golden caster sugar
60g pecan nuts, toasted on a
    baking tray in a hot oven for a
    few minutes and then chopped

To decorate
Extra orange marmalade (slightly
    warmed if difficult to spread)
Toasted pecan nuts, chopped
    (optional)

Preheat the oven to 160°C (fan)/180°C/350°F/gas mark 4 and line one 12-hole muffin tray with the appropriate size cupcake cases.

In a large mixing bowl combine the butter, corn oil, orange juice, orange zest, marmalade and vanilla extract. Set aside.

In a separate bowl, combine the flour, bicarbonate of soda and salt and set aside. Beat the eggs and sugar in a large bowl with an electric hand mixer, until the mixture is light, fluffy and quite thick. Slowly add the butter, oil and juice mixture, keeping the beater on a low speed, until it is all combined.

Add one-third of the flour mixture to the combined egg, sugar and oil mixture and beat until just combined. Pour in another third of the flour and beat again. Repeat with the last third of flour and beat until the batter just comes together. Gently fold in the pecans.

Carefully spoon the mixture evenly into the cupcakes cases, filling each one about two-thirds full. Bake in the oven for about 25 minutes, until slightly raised and golden brown. To check they are cooked, insert a skewer in the centre of one of the cakes – it should come out clean.

Remove from the oven and while the cupcakes are still warm, top each one with 1 teaspoon marmalade and spread all over the top. Sprinkle with extra pecans, if you wish. Serve immediately if possible!

Rose Cupcakes

Adorned with pale pink rose buttercream and sugared – or even fresh – rose petals, these delicately scented cupcakes are sure to inspire romance. A perfect gift for loved ones on Valentine's Day.

Makes 12 regular cupcakes

110g unsalted butter, at room
    temperature
225g caster sugar, preferably
    golden
2 large eggs, free-range or organic
150g self-raising flour, sifted
125g plain flour, sifted
½ teaspoon good-quality
    rosewater, or to taste
120ml semi-skimmed milk,
    at room temperature

To decorate
**1 batch of Rose Buttercream
    Icing (see page 49)**
**Crystallised rose petals or other
    Valentine-themed decorations**

Preheat the oven to 160°C (fan)/180°C/350°F/gas mark 4 and line a 12-hole muffin tray with the appropriate size cupcake cases.

In a large mixing bowl cream the butter and sugar until the mixture is pale and smooth, which should take 3–5 minutes using an electric hand mixer. Add the eggs, one at a time, mixing for a few minutes after each addition.

Combine the two flours in a separate bowl. Mix a little of the rosewater with the milk in a jug and test it: rosewater varies in quality and strength, so taste the mixture and adjust the amount you add accordingly. Add one-third of the flours to the creamed mixture and beat well. Pour in one-third of the milk and beat again. Repeat these steps until all the flour and milk have been added.

Carefully spoon the mixture into the cupcakes cases, filling them to about two-thirds full. Bake in the oven for about 25 minutes until slightly raised and golden brown. To check they are cooked, insert a skewer in the centre of one of the cakes – it should come out clean.

Remove from the oven and leave the cakes in their tins for about 10 minutes before carefully placing on a wire rack to cool. Once they are completely cool, ice with rose buttercream and sprinkle with your choice of decorations – crystallised rose petals, sugar hearts, sugar flowers, hundreds and thousands – it's up to you!

Rose Buttercream Icing

This buttercream, infused with rosewater, is simply adapted from our classic vanilla buttercream. By adding the rosewater carefully you can produce a subtle or stronger flavour, depending on your preference. Perfect on our rose cupcakes (see page 46), this icing could also be used on vanilla (see page 15) or orange sponge cupcakes (see page 52).

In a large mixing bowl beat the butter, milk, vanilla extract and half the icing sugar until smooth – this can take several minutes using an electric hand mixer. Gradually add the remainder of the icing sugar and beat again until the buttercream is smooth and creamy. Add the rosewater at the very end and beat thoroughly, tasting to check if it is scented enough.

To colour, simply beat in a tiny drop of pink food colouring.

Makes enough to ice 15–20 regular or 60 mini cupcakes

115g unsalted butter, at room temperature
4 tablespoons semi-skimmed milk, at room temperature
1 teaspoon vanilla extract
500g icing sugar, sifted
½ teaspoon good-quality rosewater, or to taste
Pink food colouring (optional)

Chocolate Liqueur Cupcakes

As an alternative to the more delicate rose cupcakes, these rich chocolate truffle and liqueur cupcakes make an indulgent Valentine's present. We have suggested champagne truffles to decorate but almost any variety of truffle would work equally well.

Make the chocolate cupcakes in the usual way, but use only 90ml milk and mix with the framboise.

When the cupcakes are completely cool, ice them with the chocolate buttercream icing, then place a champagne truffle in the centre of each one. Press down gently so that the truffle does not roll off.

Makes 16 regular cupcakes

**1 batch of Chocolate Cupcakes
  (see page 16)**
**2 tablespoons framboise
  (raspberry liqueur)**

To decorate
**1 batch of Chocolate Buttercream
  Icing (see page 29)**
16 champagne truffles

Orange Cupcakes

You could make these cupcakes for an afternoon tea on Mother's Day. Serve them on pretty vintage china with fresh spring flowers and maybe a cup of fragranced tea, such as jasmine or lapsang souchong.

Makes 12 regular cupcakes

110g unsalted butter, at room temperature
225g caster sugar, preferably golden
2 large eggs, free-range or organic
150g self-raising flour, sifted
125g plain flour, sifted
90ml semi-skimmed milk, at room temperature
2 tablespoons freshly squeezed orange juice
Grated zest of 1 orange (you need 1 teaspoon)

To decorate
1 batch of Orange Blossom Buttercream Icing (see opposite)
Orange sugar flowers

Preheat the oven to 160°C (fan)/180°C/350°F/gas mark 4 and line a 12-hole muffin tray with the appropriate size cupcake cases.

In a large mixing bowl cream the butter and sugar until the mixture is pale and smooth, which should take 3–5 minutes using an electric hand mixer Add the eggs, one at a time, mixing for a few minutes after each addition.

Combine the two flours in a separate bowl. Add one-third of the flours to the creamed mixture and beat well. Pour in half the milk and beat well. Add another third of the flour and beat again. Beat in the remainder of the milk and all the orange juice. Finish by adding the last third of the flour and the orange zest and beat well. If the mixture looks like it is curdling slightly, don't panic – simply add another spoonful of plain flour and beat well.

Carefully spoon the mixture into the cupcake cases, filling them to about two-thirds full. Bake in the oven for about 25 minutes until lightly golden brown. To check they are cooked, insert a skewer in the centre of one of the cakes – it should come out clean.

Remove from the oven and leave the cakes in their tins for about 10 minutes before carefully placing on a wire rack to cool. Once they are completely cool, ice with orange blossom buttercream icing and decorate decorate with either an orange sugar flower, orange zest or, if you are lucky enough to find any, some fresh orange blossom flowers.

Orange Blossom Buttercream Icing

In a large mixing bowl beat the butter, juice and half the icing sugar until smooth – this can take several minutes using an electric hand mixer. Gradually add the remainder of the icing sugar and beat until smooth and creamy. Add the orange blossom water and beat again. Taste the icing to see if it is flavoured enough and if necessary add a little more of the orange blossom water.

Makes enough to ice
12–15 regular cupcakes

115g unsalted butter, at room temperature
2 tablespoons freshly squeezed orange juice
500g icing sugar, sifted
1–2 teaspoons orange blossom water (try to find a fairly concentrated one – available in the supermarket baking aisle)

Earl Grey Cupcakes

The delicate bergamot flavour of Earl Grey tea will intensify with every bite here. If you are a tea lover and have a fondness for a particular blend, you could easily substitute that one. We think these cupcakes make an ideal Mother's Day treat as they look so pretty piled on a plate at the centre of a special afternoon tea.

Makes about
12 regular cupcakes

125ml semi-skimmed milk,
    at room temperature
4 Earl Grey teabags
110g unsalted butter, at room
    temperature
225g granulated sugar
½ teaspoon almond extract
    (optional)
2 large eggs, free-range or organic
125g self-raising flour, sifted
120g plain flour, sifted

To decorate (optional)
1 batch of Vanilla Buttercream
    Icing (see page 26),
    coloured lilac
Granulated sugar or
    sugar flowers

Preheat the oven to 160°C (fan)/180°C/350°F/gas mark 4 and line a 12-hole muffin tray with the appropriate size cupcake cases.

Heat the milk in a saucepan over a medium heat until it just begins to boil. Remove from the heat and add the teabags. Cover with clingfilm and leave to infuse for about 30 minutes, then discard the teabags.

In a large mixing bowl cream the butter and sugar until the mixture is pale and smooth, which should take 3–5 minutes using an electric hand mixer. Add the almond extract, if using, and the eggs, one at a time, mixing for a few minutes after each addition.

Combine the two flours in a separate bowl. Add one-third of the flours to the creamed mixture and beat well. Pour in one-third of the infused milk and beat again. Repeat these steps until all the flour and milk have been added.

Carefully spoon the mixture into the cupcake cases, filling them to about two-thirds full. Bake in the oven for about 25 minutes until slightly raised and golden brown. To check they are cooked, insert a skewer in the centre of one of the cakes – it should come out clean.

Remove from the oven and leave the cakes in their tins for about 10 minutes before carefully placing on a wire rack to cool. Once they are completely cool, you could ice the cupcakes with lilac-coloured vanilla buttercream and sprinkle with a little extra granulated sugar and sugar flowers.

Coffee Cupcakes

You will find no coffee essence here – these are the real deal with a full kick of espresso powder. They make a delicious Mother's Day gift or, in mini size, an after-dinner treat. Topped with crushed walnuts or chocolate-covered espresso beans, these are cupcakes for grown-ups.

Preheat the oven to 160°C (fan)/180°C/350°F/gas mark 4 and line a 12-hole muffin tray or three 12-hole mini muffin trays with the appropriate size cupcake cases.

In a large mixing bowl cream the butter and sugars until the mixture is pale and smooth, which should take 3–5 minutes using an electric hand mixer. Add the eggs, one at a time, mixing for a few minutes after each addition. Do not worry if the mixture splits a bit after adding the eggs – this will not affect the outcome.

Combine the flours in a separate bowl. Mix the vanilla extract and espresso powder with the milk in a jug and stir to combine. Add one-third of the flours to the creamed mixture and beat well. Pour in one-third of the milk and beat again. Repeat these steps until all the flour and milk have been added.

Carefully spoon the mixture into the cupcake cases, filling them to about two-thirds full. Bake in the oven for about 25 minutes (regular size) or 15 minutes (mini size) until slightly raised and golden brown. To check they are cooked, insert a skewer in the centre of one of the cakes – it should come out clean.

Remove from the oven and leave the cakes in their tins for about 10 minutes before carefully placing on a wire rack to cool.

Once they are completely cool, ice with coffee buttercream and decorate with either whole or crushed walnuts or chocolate-covered espresso beans.

Makes 12 regular or
36 mini cupcakes

**110g unsalted butter, at
    room temperature**
110g demerara sugar
120g light soft brown sugar
2 large eggs, free-range or organic
125g self-raising flour, sifted
120g plain flour, sifted
**¼ teaspoon good-quality
    vanilla extract**
**1 tablespoon instant
    espresso powder**
**125ml semi-skimmed milk, at
    room temperature**

To decorate
**1 batch of Coffee Buttercream
    Icing (see page 32)**
**Walnuts or chocolate-covered
    espresso beans**

Mars Bar Cupcakes

These are an extremely rich Easter treat, hugely popular with adults and children alike. They are not really cupcakes, but are incredibly easy to make and look great with Easter decorations. It is surprisingly hard to resist eating more than one!

Makes about 10 regular or
30 mini cupcakes

**50g unsalted butter, at
room temperature**
2 tablespoons golden syrup
**260g Mars bars, chopped into
1cm square pieces**
150g cornflakes

To decorate
**1 batch of Chocolate Buttercream
Icing (see page 29)**
**Easter chicks or rabbits or small
chocolate eggs**

Line a 12-hole muffin tray or three 12-hole mini muffin trays with the appropriate size cupcake cases.

Melt the butter and golden syrup in a saucepan over a very low heat, stirring constantly. Add the chopped Mars bars and keep stirring until just melted. Remove from the heat and gently fold in the cornflakes completely – although don't mix too forcefully or you will crush the cornflakes.

Press a spoonful of the mix loosely into each cupcake case and leave them to cool and set. When they are completely cool, put a small amount of chocolate buttercream icing in the centre of each cupcake and decorate with an Easter chick or rabbit or a small chocolate egg.

Should there be any uneaten, the cupcakes can be stored in an airtight container for about 3 days.

Caramel Cupcakes

An equally rich alternative to our other Easter cupcakes, these would also be delicious on a cold winter's day and, once iced with our caramel buttercream icing, could be decorated with almost any crunchy chocolate or toffee pieces.

Preheat the oven to 160°C (fan)/180°C/350°F/gas mark 4 and line a 12-hole muffin tray or three 12-hole mini muffin trays with the appropriate size cupcake cases. If making your own caramel sauce, make it first as it needs to cool before you use it.

In a large mixing bowl cream the butter and sugars until pale and smooth, which should take about 3–5 minutes using an electric hand mixer. Add the eggs, one at a time, mixing for a few minutes after each addition. Add the vanilla extract.

Combine the flours in a separate bowl. Add one-third of the flours to the creamed mixture and mix until the batter just comes together. Add the caramel sauce and beat well. Add another third of the flour and beat until it just comes together. Add the double cream and again beat well. Add the remaining flour and beat until the mixture is combined.

Carefully spoon the mixture into the cupcake cases, filling them to about two-thirds full. Bake in the oven for about 25 minutes until slightly raised and golden brown. To check they are cooked, insert a skewer in the centre of one of the cakes – it should come out clean.

Remove from the oven and leave the cakes in their tins for about 10 minutes before carefully placing on a wire rack to cool.

Once they are completely cool, ice with caramel buttercream icing. Crush a couple of Dime bars and sprinkle over the cupcakes.

Makes 12 regular cupcakes

110g unsalted butter, at room temperature
120g light soft brown sugar
120g dark soft brown sugar
2 large eggs, free-range or organic
½ teaspoon good-quality vanilla extract
125g self-raising flour, sifted
120g plain flour, sifted
75ml caramel sauce, ready-made (there is a brand called Vatrine, which is black in colour), or see page 64
50ml double cream

To decorate
1 batch of Caramel Buttercream Icing (see page 65)
A couple of Dime bars

Caramel Sauce

This makes about 75ml – enough to use in the caramel cupcakes (see page 63).

250g golden caster sugar
135ml water

Put the sugar and 5 tablespoons of the measured water in a heavy saucepan and stir over a low heat until the sugar has dissolved. Increase the heat and cook over a high heat for about 10 minutes, after which the mixture should be dark amber in colour.

Remove the pan from the heat and leave to cool slightly. Stir gently to help it cool but take great care as the sugar is extremely hot – this might be best done by holding the pan away from you over a sink.

Once the mixture has cooled slightly, add the remaining water to the mix and continue stirring. Again hold the pan away from you when adding the water as it may spatter.

When the sauce is completely cool, pour into a bowl and cover until ready to use. Any unused sauce can be stored in an airtight container for up to a week.

Caramel Buttercream Icing

This buttercream works well with the caramel cupcakes (see page 63) or the chocolate cupcakes (see page 16), although it will take slightly more patience and care than others. Pay particular attention not to burn yourself but it is well worth the effort and we highly recommend it!

Place the butter, milk and brown sugar in a heavy saucepan over a high heat and stir to combine. Bring to the boil, stirring continuously, and allow it to boil for 1 minute.

Remove from the heat and stir in half of the icing sugar. Leave the mixture to cool slightly, then add the remainder of the icing sugar and the vanilla extract and stir until it thickens to the desired consistency.

This icing is best used immediately. If you do need to make it in advance, or if you have some left over, thin it with a little double cream and beat well before using. Alternatively, heat the icing for 10 seconds in a microwave.

Makes enough to ice
12 regular cupcakes

60g unsalted butter, at room temperature
6 tablespoons milk, at room temperature
220g light, soft brown sugar
240g icing sugar, sifted
½ teaspoon good-quality vanilla extract
Double cream, as needed

Malted Cupcakes

These malt-flavoured cupcakes are perfect for children to help bake, give and then share with their dads come Father's Day. Ice with marshmallow icing or chocolate buttercream. Exceedingly tasty, with a pinch of nostalgia!

Makes 12 regular cupcakes

110g unsalted butter, at room temperature
120g light soft brown sugar
100g caster sugar, preferably golden
2 large eggs, free-range or organic
125g self-raising flour, sifted
60g plain flour, sifted
50g Ovaltine (malted drink) powder
125ml semi-skimmed milk , at room temperature
½ teaspoon good-quality vanilla extract
1 tablespoon sour cream

To decorate
1 batch of Marshmallow Icing (see page 69) or Chocolate Buttercream Icing (see page 29)
Maltesers or extra Ovaltine powder

Preheat the oven to 160°C (fan)/180°C/350°F/gas mark 4 and line a 12-hole muffin tray with the appropriate size cupcake cases.

In a large mixing bowl cream the butter and sugars until pale and smooth, which should take about 3–5 minutes using an electric hand mixer. Add the eggs, one at a time, mixing for a few minutes after each addition.

Combine the flours and Ovaltine in a separate bowl. Mix the milk, vanilla extract and sour cream in a jug. Add one-third of the flour and Ovaltine mixture to the creamed mixture and beat well. Pour in one-third of the milk and beat again. Repeat these steps until all the flour mixture and milk have been added.

Carefully spoon the mixture into the cupcake cases, filling them to about two-thirds full. Bake in the oven for about 25 minutes until slightly raised and golden brown. To check they are cooked, insert a skewer in the centre of one of the cakes – it should come out clean.

Remove from the oven and leave the cakes in their tins for about 10 minutes before carefully placing on a wire rack to cool.

Once they are completely cool, ice these cupcakes with chocolate buttercream or marshmallow icing and decorate with whole or crushed Maltesers or a simple sprinkling of Ovaltine. For a lucky father, you could use some sugar lettering to spell out 'daddy' on one of them or write it using an icing tube or pen available in many colours in supermarkets.

Marshmallow Icing

Please note that this icing is easiest to work with while it is still slightly warm, so try to use it immediately. As it has a very sticky consistency, you may find it a little harder to ice with than most of our icings, but be patient and persevere! Any left over can be kept in the fridge overnight, but we would not recommend keeping this icing for long if it is not used.

Cook the sugar, golden syrup and water in a saucepan over a high heat until the mixture reaches the soft-ball stage (115°C/239°F) on a sugar thermometer, which should take about 6 minutes. Remove from the heat.

Meanwhile, in a clean bowl whisk the egg whites with an electric hand mixer until soft peaks start to form. With the blades still beating on a low speed, slowly pour the hot sugar syrup in a steady stream on to the egg whites. Continue to beat on a low speed until all the hot syrup is in the mixing bowl.

Increase the speed to medium-high and continue beating the mixture until it becomes thick, glossy and cool. Add the vanilla extract, if using, towards the end of the mixing process.

Makes enough to ice 12 regular cupcakes with some left over

120g granulated sugar
80g golden syrup
1½ tablespoons water
2 large egg whites, free-range
   or organic
½ teaspoon good-quality
   vanilla extract (optional)

Peanut Butter Cupcakes

This is a fairly dense and rich cupcake. However, a batch is too good to make only for July 4th! It can be tricky to find the peanut butter chips we recommend for decoration, but more specialist food shops or American delis should stock them. Altenatively, use Reeses pieces.

Makes 12 regular cupcakes

75g unsalted butter, at room temperature
130g smooth peanut butter
190g dark soft brown sugar
2 large eggs, free-range or organic
1 teaspoon good-quality vanilla extract
120g plain flour, sifted
1 teaspoon baking powder
Pinch of salt
60ml semi-skimmed milk, at room temperature

To decorate
1 batch of Milk Chocolate Icing (see page 72)
Peanut butter or milk chocolate chips

Preheat the oven to 160°C (fan)/180°C/350°F/gas mark 4 and line a 12-hole muffin tray with the appropriate size cupcake cases.

In a large mixing bowl cream the butter, peanut butter and sugar until well blended. Add the eggs, one at a time, mixing for a few minutes after each addition, and then stir in the vanilla extract.

Combine the flour, baking powder and salt in a separate bowl. Add one-third of the flour to the creamed mixture and beat well. Pour in one-third of the milk and beat again. Repeat these steps until all the flour mixture and milk have been added.

Carefully spoon the mixture into the cupcake cases, filling them to about two-thirds full. Bake in the oven for about 20 minutes until slightly raised and golden brown. To check they are cooked, insert a skewer in the centre of one of the cakes – it should come out clean.

Remove from the oven and leave the cakes in their tins for about 10 minutes before carefully placing on a wire rack to cool.

Once they are completely cool, ice with milk chocolate icing. Top with peanut butter chips if you can find them, or milk chocolate chips, and don't forget your American flag if it's Independence Day.

Milk Chocolate Icing

We use this icing specifically for our peanut butter cupcakes (see page 70) as we think it works better with this particular flavour of sponge than our buttercream icing and sometimes makes a nice change – it is considerably more fiddly to make but tastes delicious! By all means try it out on some of the other cupcakes – vanilla or chocolate sponge maybe?

Makes enough to ice
12 regular cupcakes

60ml double cream
30g unsalted butter, at
   room temperature
300g good-quality milk chocolate,
   broken into small pieces
½ teaspoon good-quality
   vanilla extract

Put the double cream and butter in a saucepan over a very low heat. Stir the mixture continuously and do not let it come to the boil or it will burn. As soon as the butter has completely melted, remove from the heat and add the chocolate. Allow the chocolate to melt in the pan, which may take up to 10 minutes, during which time you should keep stirring the mixture continuously. If any chocolate does not melt, return the pan to a very low heat and let it melt. Add the vanilla extract and stir again.

If the icing is too runny to use, allow it to remain at room temperature for a while, then beat just before you start to decorate your cupcakes. Any unused icing should be stored in a container in the fridge.

Strawberries and Cream Cupcakes

Primrose Bakery always uses seasonal fruit. So when summer is upon us, these are the cupcakes, preferably made with the sweetest and juiciest English strawberries, that fill our counters. This recipe is easiest made in a food processor, but you can still make it with an electric hand mixer.

Preheat the oven to 160°C (fan)/180°C/350°F/gas mark 4 and line a 12-hole muffin tray with the appropriate size cupcake cases.

Put the sugar, flour, baking powder, cornflour and crushed strawberries into a food processor. Pulse until evenly mixed (roughly 4 seconds). Add the butter and eggs and process briefly until even (roughly 10 seconds). If you are using an electric hand mixer, cream the butter and sugar together first, beat in the eggs, one by one, and then add the remaining ingredients and beat well together.

Carefully spoon the mixture into the cupcake cases, filling them to about two-thirds full. Bake in the oven for about 25 minutes. The cakes will be fairly moist even when cooked.

Remove from the oven and leave the cakes in their tins for about 10 minutes before carefully placing on a wire rack to cool.

Once they are completely cool, carefully make a small hole in the centre of each cupcake and use a teaspoon to push the strawberry jam into the hole – you can slightly warm the jam in a saucepan first to soften it before pushing it into the sponge.

Wash the 12 strawberries and allow them to dry off on kitchen paper to limit any excess water and juice spoiling the buttercream once they are on the cupcakes. Decorate the cupcakes with vanilla buttercream icing and, just before serving, place a fresh strawberry in the centre.

Makes 12 regular cupcakes

225g caster sugar
210g self-raising flour, sifted
1 teaspoon baking powder
25g cornflour
125g fresh, ripe strawberries, hulled and crushed
225g unsalted butter, at room temperature
4 large eggs, free-range or organic

To decorate
Good-quality strawberry jam (1 teaspoon for each cupcake)
1 batch of Vanilla Buttercream Icing (see page 26)
12 small strawberries

Coconut Cupcakes with Pink Vanilla Buttercream

If coconut ice is your thing, these are going to be your ideal cupcake. Filled with moist coconut, encased in vanilla sponge, topped with a delicate pink icing and coconut shavings …a sweet treat in cupcake form.

Makes 12 regular cupcakes

110g unsalted butter, at room
    temperature
180g caster sugar
2 large eggs, free-range or organic
½ teaspoon good-quality
    vanilla extract
⅛ teaspoon almond extract
    (optional)
125g self-raising flour, sifted
120g plain flour, sifted
125ml coconut milk
25g desiccated coconut

To decorate
1 batch of Vanilla Buttercream
    Icing (see page 26), coloured
    pale pink
Coconut flakes, lightly toasted in
    the oven for a few minutes

Preheat the oven to 160°C (fan)/180°C/350°F/gas mark 4 and line a 12-hole muffin tray with the appropriate size cupcake cases.

In a large mixing bowl cream the butter and sugar until pale and smooth, which should take about 3–5 minutes using an electric hand mixer. Add the eggs, one at a time, mixing for a few minutes after each addition and adding the vanilla and almond extract (if using) at the end.

Combine the two flours in a separate bowl. Add one-third of the flours to the creamed mixture and beat well. Pour in one-third of the coconut milk and beat again. Repeat these steps until all the flour and milk have been added. Fold in the desiccated coconut using a metal spoon.

Carefully spoon the mixture into the cupcake cases, filling them to about two-thirds full. Bake in the oven for about 25 minutes until slightly raised and golden brown. To check they are cooked, insert a skewer in the centre of one of the cakes – it should come out clean.

Remove from the oven and leave the cakes in their tins for about 10 minutes before carefully placing on a wire rack to cool.

Once they are completely cool, ice the cupcakes with pink-tinted vanilla buttercream and sprinkle a few toasted coconut flakes over each one.

Raspberry Cupcakes

A perfect summer combination: fresh, tart raspberries and sweet, creamy white chocolate buttercream. Putting the raspberry jam directly into the sponge once it's cooked makes the cupcakes look very pretty when cut open and the combination of tastes is divine. You could decorate them with some whole raspberries and serve with iced tea or fresh lemonade at a picnic or afternoon tea.

Preheat the oven to 160°C (fan)/180°C/350°F/gas mark 4 and line a 12-hole muffin tray or three 12-hole mini muffin trays with the appropriate size cupcake cases.

In a large mixing bowl cream the butter and sugar until pale and smooth, which should take about 3–5 minutes using an electric beater. Add the eggs, one at a time, mixing for a few minutes after each addition.

Combine the two flours in a separate bowl. Put the milk in a jug and add the vanilla extract to it. Add one-third of the flours to the creamed mixture and beat well. Pour in one-third of the milk and beat again. Repeat these steps until all the flour and milk have been added.

Gently fold in the raspberry jam until most of it is combined. The idea is to have some jam streaks running through the mixture, rather than an evenly coloured batter. Carefully spoon the mixture into the cupcake cases, filling them to about two-thirds full. Bake in the oven for about 25 minutes until slightly raised and golden brown.

Remove from the oven and leave the cakes in their tins for about 10 minutes before carefully placing on a wire rack to cool. Once they have cooled, cut a small hole in the centre of each cake using a sharp knife or teaspoon and carefully place a teaspoon of jam inside – you can slightly warm the jam in a saucepan first to soften it before pushing it into the sponge.

Ice the cupcakes with white chocolate buttercream and decorate with fresh whole raspberries.

Makes 12 regular cupcakes

110g unsalted butter, at room
    temperature
180g caster sugar
2 large eggs, free-range or organic
125g self-raising flour, sifted
120g plain flour, sifted
125ml semi-skimmed milk, at
    room temperature
1 teaspoon good-quality
    vanilla extract
3 tablespoons good-quality
    seedless raspberry jam

To decorate
Good-quality raspberry jam
    (1 teaspoon for each cupcake)
1 batch of White Chocolate
    Buttercream Icing
    (see page 80)
Fresh raspberries (2 for
    each cupcake)

White Chocolate Buttercream Icing

This sweet white chocolate buttercream works brilliantly with the raspberry cupcakes (see page 79) but you could just as well add a swirl of it to the chocolate, strawberry or coconut ones.

**Makes enough to ice
12 regular or 36 mini cupcakes**

**100g good-quality white
   chocolate, broken into pieces
60g (4 tablespoons) Vanilla
   Buttercream Icing
   (see page 26)
3 tablespoons double cream**

To melt the chocolate, put it in a jug in a microwave on a medium heat for 30 seconds, stir and then microwave for a further 30 seconds – but be careful not to burn the chocolate. Alternatively, put the pieces in a heatproof bowl over a saucepan of barely simmering water. Stir occasionally until it has completely melted and is quite smooth. Leave to cool slightly.

Once the chocolate has cooled, combine all the ingredients and beat well until smooth and creamy. It is best to use this icing immediately. If it begins to stiffen too much, soften with a little more double cream or heat in the microwave for 10 seconds, beating well again before using.

This icing needs to be stored in the fridge because it contains cream and will need to be beaten well again before use if it has become too cold and stiff.

Ginger Cupcakes

With the bite of ginger and black treacle, these make great Halloween or winter treats. Be generous with ginger fudge icing to top the cakes and let your Halloween imagination go wild!

Preheat the oven to 160°C (fan)/180°C/350°F/gas mark 4 and line two 12-hole muffin trays with the appropriate size and number of cupcake cases.

Melt the butter, sugar and treacle in a saucepan over a low heat. Cool briefly and then stir in the milk.

Add the chopped ginger to the beaten eggs and then beat into the butter mixture. Sift the flour, ground ginger and salt and add to the warm mixture. Combine thoroughly.

Carefully spoon the mixture into the cupcake cases, filling them to about two-thirds full. Bake in the oven for 30–35 minutes. To check they are cooked, insert a skewer in the centre of one of the cakes – it should come out clean.

Remove from the oven and leave the cakes in their tins for about 10 minutes before carefully placing on a wire rack to cool. Once they are completely cool, ice each cake generously with ginger fudge icing then add your Halloween decorations – the scarier the better! Or you could simply top each one with a sprinkling of demerara sugar over the icing.

These cupcakes are best eaten when they are freshly made; they tend to dry out a little more quickly than some of our other cupcakes.

Makes 18 regular cupcakes

200g unsalted butter, diced, at room temperature
175g dark soft brown sugar
3 tablespoons black treacle (molasses)
150ml semi-skimmed milk, at room temperature
4 pieces of stem ginger, drained and chopped (reserve the syrup for the ginger fudge icing)
2 large eggs, free-range or organic, beaten
300g self-raising flour, sifted
1 tablespoon ground ginger
Pinch of salt

To decorate
1 batch Ginger Fudge Icing (see page 84)
Halloween decorations of your choice or demerara sugar

Ginger Fudge Icing

This spicy icing is the perfect creamy topping for the dark and dense ginger cupcakes (see page 83) – a really flavour-packed combination to devour behind closed doors or to hand out to trick-or-treaters.

Makes enough to ice
18 regular cupcakes

**140g unsalted butter, at room
temperature**
**2 teaspoons freshly squeezed
lemon juice**
**4 tablespoons ginger syrup,
drained from a jar of
stem ginger**
300g icing sugar, sifted

In a large mixing bowl beat the butter for a few minutes until really smooth, then add the remaining ingredients and beat again until the icing is smooth and creamy.

Pumpkin Cupcakes

Less sweet and a little spicier than some of our other cupcake recipes, these would work their magic before a night of trick-and-treating and the inevitable basket of sweets that comes home afterwards! If you can't find puréed pumpkin, cut a butternut squash into pieces, de-seed and steam for about 30 minutes. Then mash, pass through a sieve and leave to drain for several hours to get rid of the excess water.

Makes 12 regular cupcakes

110g unsalted butter, at
    room temperature
240g soft light brown sugar
2 large eggs, free-range or organic
½ teaspoon good-quality
    vanilla extract
100g puréed pumpkin (sold
    in tins)
125g self-raising flour, sifted
120g plain flour, sifted
½ teaspoon ground cinnamon
½ teaspoon ground ginger
125ml buttermilk (or
    120ml milk mixed with
    1 teaspoon lemon juice)

To decorate
1 batch of Spiced Cream Cheese
    Icing (see page 87)
Ground cinnamon, grated
    nutmeg or Halloween
    decorations of your choice

Preheat the oven to 160°C (fan)/180°C/350°F/gas mark 4 and line a 12-hole muffin tray with the appropriate size cupcake cases.

In a large mixing bowl cream the butter and sugar until the mixture is pale and smooth, which should take about 3–5 minutes using an electric hand mixer. Add the eggs, one at a time, and the vanilla extract, beating well after each addition. Add the pumpkin and beat until just combined.

Combine the flours, cinnamon and ginger in a bowl. Add one-third of the flours to the creamed mixture and beat until just combined. Add half of the buttermilk and beat again until just combined. Repeat these steps until all the flour and buttermilk have been added.

Carefully spoon the mixture into the cupcake cases, filling them to about two-thirds full. Bake in the oven for about 25 minutes until slightly raised and golden brown. To check they are cooked, insert a skewer in the centre of one of the cakes – it should come out clean.

Remove from the oven and leave the cakes in their tins for about 10 minutes before placing carefully on a wire rack to cool.

Once they are completely cool, ice the cupcakes with spiced cream cheese icing and decorate with a sprinkling of cinnamon or nutmeg on the top or some Halloween decorations, if that's the occasion.

Spiced Cream Cheese Icing

A simple variation on the orange cream cheese icing from earlier in the book, this one could also work well with the carrot cupcakes (see page 21) but is especially delicious with the pumpkin cupcakes on a cold and windy Halloween night.

Place all the ingredients in a mixing bowl and beat well until thoroughly combined and the icing is smooth and pale.

This icing must be stored in the fridge as it contains cream cheese, but will keep well. Before re-using, let it come to room temperature and then beat again.

Makes enough to ice
about 15 regular cupcakes

175g cream cheese
450g icing sugar, sifted
125g unsalted butter, at room
    temperature
¼ teaspoon ground cinnamon
Pinch of ground cloves

Chocolate and Banana Cupcakes

A good recipe for afternoon tea round the fire on a wet or chilly day. These cupcakes use our chocolate buttercream for their icing, which really brings out the flavour of the chocolate chips in the sponge.

Makes 12 regular cupcakes

125g unsalted butter, at room temperature
250g caster sugar
2 eggs, free-range or organic, lightly beaten
1 teaspoon good-quality vanilla extract
250g plain flour, sifted
2 teaspoons baking powder
4 ripe bananas, mashed with a fork
175g good-quality dark chocolate (70% cocoa solids), broken or chopped into small pieces

To decorate (optional)
1 batch of Chocolate Buttercream Icing (see page 29)
Chopped walnuts

Preheat the oven to 160°C (fan)/180°C/350°F/gas mark 4 and line a 12-hole muffin tray with the appropriate size cupcake cases.

In a large mixing bowl cream the butter and sugar until the mixture is pale and smooth, which should take 3–5 minutes using an electric hand mixer. Add the eggs and vanilla extract and beat again briefly. Add the flour and baking powder and beat again until well combined. Stir in the mashed bananas and chocolate pieces using a wooden spoon.

Carefully spoon the mixture into the cupcake cases, filling them to about two-thirds full. Bake in the oven for about 25 minutes. To check they are cooked, insert a skewer in the centre of one of the cakes – it should come out clean.

Remove from the oven and leave the cakes in their tins for about 10 minutes before carefully placing on a wire rack to cool.

Once they are completely cool, ice the cupcakes with chocolate buttercream. If you wish, pop some chopped walnuts on each one. Alternatively you could simply serve them with no icing at all for a breakfast treat, warmed in the oven for a few minutes beforehand.

Chocolate-Orange Cupcakes

It is well established that the combination of orange and chocolate is a delectable union, so we have put this to good use with this cupcake recipe. The rich flavours of chocolate and seasonal ripe oranges make it a winter winner.

Preheat the oven to 160°C (fan)/180°C/350°F/gas mark 4 and line a 12-hole muffin tray with the appropriate size cupcake cases.

Break the chocolate into pieces and place in a microwave-safe bowl. Melt on a medium setting in 30-second bursts until completely melted. Stir well between each session. Alternatively, place the chocolate in a heatproof bowl over a saucepan of barely simmering water. Stir occasionally until completely melted. Set the bowl aside to cool.

In a large mixing bowl cream the butter, sugar and orange zest until the mixture is pale and smooth, which should take 3–5 minutes using an electric hand mixer. Add the eggs and beat again briefly.

Combine the flour, bicarbonate of soda, baking powder and salt in a bowl. Mix the milk and orange juice in a jug.

Add the chocolate to the creamed mixture and beat on a low speed until the mixture is just combined. The batter will still be streaky. Add one-third of the flour mix and beat until it all just comes together. Add half of the juice/milk mix and beat again until the mixture just comes together. Repeat these steps until all the ingredients have been incorporated.

Carefully spoon the mixture into the cupcake cases, filling them to about two-thirds full. Bake in the oven for about 28–30 minutes. To check they are cooked, insert a skewer in the centre of one of the cakes – it should come out clean.

Remove from the oven and leave the cakes in their tins for about 10 minutes before carefully placing on a wire rack to cool. Once they are completely cool, ice the cupcakes with chocolate buttercream and decorate with a little orange zest or sugar flowers.

Makes 12 regular cupcakes

115g good-quality dark
    chocolate (70% cocoa solids)
90g unsalted butter, at room
    temperature
175g caster sugar, preferably
    golden
Grated zest and juice of 1 orange
    (you need 75ml of juice)
2 large eggs, free-range or organic
185g plain flour, sifted
½ teaspoon bicarbonate of soda
½ teaspoon baking powder
½ teaspoon salt
1 tablespoon semi-skimmed milk,
    at room temperature

To decorate
1 batch of Chocolate Buttercream
    Icing (see page 29)
Grated orange zest or
    sugar flowers

Cranberry and Orange Cupcakes

These distinctively tangy cupcakes are delicious just baked and served warm, or try them topped with our orange blossom buttercream (see page 53) or orange cream cheese icing (see page 35) as a healthier alternative to all the rich food around during the Christmas period.

Makes 12 regular or
36 mini cupcakes

2 large eggs, free-range or organic
200g caster sugar
100g corn oil
135ml sour cream
1 teaspoon good-quality
**   vanilla extract**
Grated zest of 1 orange (you
**   need 1 teaspoon)**
228g plain flour
½ teaspoon baking powder
¼ teaspoon bicarbonate of soda
¼ teaspoon salt
1 teaspoon ground cinnamon
140g fresh or frozen
**   cranberries, finely chopped**

To decorate
1 batch of Orange Blossom
**   Buttercream Icing (see page**
**   53) or Orange Cream**
**   Cheese Icing (see page 35)**
Whole fresh or dried cranberries
**   or Christmas-themed**
**   decorations**

Preheat the oven to 140°C (fan)/150°C/300°F/gas mark 2 and line a 12-hole muffin tray or three 12-hole mini muffin trays with the appropriate size cupcake cases.

In a large mixing bowl beat the eggs and sugar together until light and fluffy, which should take 3–5 minutes using an electric hand mixer. Slowly pour in the oil, a little at a time, beating well after each addition, then repeat the process with the sour cream and vanilla extract, making sure everything is well combined, and incorporate the orange zest at the end.

Sift the dry ingredients together in a bowl and then add to the batter and beat well. Finally, fold in the cranberries gently.

Carefully spoon the mixture into the cupcake cases, filling them to about two-thirds full. Bake in the oven for about 25 minutes (regular size) or 15 minutes (mini size) until slightly raised and golden brown. To check they are cooked, insert a skewer in the centre of one of the cakes – it should come out clean.

Allow to cool in their tins for 10 minutes or so before turning out on to a wire rack to cool. Once they are completely cool, ice with either orange blossom buttercream or orange cream cheese icing and decorate with whole fresh or dried cranberries or some Christmas-themed decorations.

Peppermint Buttercream Icing

As Christmas is upon us once again, this peppermint buttercream fits perfectly with the season's festivities. Team with chocolate cupcakes (see page 16) and top with crushed stripey candy – the mint chocolate cupcakes will sit proudly next to plates of mince pies at any occasion.

Makes enough to ice
15–20 regular or about
60 mini cupcakes

110g unsalted butter, at room temperature
60ml semi-skimmed milk, at room temperature
½ teaspoon good-quality peppermint extract (or more or less, depending on how minty you want your icing)
500g icing sugar, sifted
Few drops of green food colouring

To decorate
Chocolate chips, candy canes or striped peppermints

In a large mixing bowl beat the butter, milk, peppermint extract and half the icing sugar until smooth – this can take several minutes using an electric hand mixer. Gradually add the remainder of the icing sugar and beat again until the buttercream is smooth and creamy. Taste the icing at this stage to see if you want to add more peppermint extract.

Add a drop of green colouring and beat thoroughly. This will be all you need to achieve a very pale pastel hue. Add carefully, drop by drop, and beat after each addition to build up to your desired shade.

Use the icing to decorate chocolate cupcakes. Top with some chocolate chips or crush some candy canes or striped peppermints and sprinkle over each cupcake.

Brandy Buttercream Icing

As an alternative to the traditional Christmas cake, brandy buttercream icing could be used on either chocolate cupcakes or a chocolate layer cake. Either would be perfect served at a Christmas party with a glass of champagne.

In a large mixing bowl beat the butter, milk, brandy butter, vanilla extract and half the icing sugar until smooth – this can take a few minutes using an electric hand mixer. Gradually add the remainder of the icing sugar until creamy and smooth.

Taste the buttercream to check if there is enough brandy butter, if necessary adding a little more, although remember how rich brandy butter is, especially combined with chocolate sponge, so don't add too much!

Ice up a batch of chocolate cupcakes and then finish off with a brandy or cognac truffle or some pretty Christmas decoration.

The buttercream can be stored in an airtight container for up to 3 days at room temperature. Before re-using beat well.

Makes enough to ice
15–20 regular cupcakes

115g unsalted butter, at room
    temperature
60ml semi-skimmed milk, at
    room temperature
2 big tablespoons good-quality
    brandy butter
1 teaspoon good-quality
    vanilla extract
500g icing sugar, sifted

To decorate
Cognac or Brandy truffles

tip

If you decide to use this icing on a chocolate layer cake (see page 128), it might work better if it were used in the middle layer only and then the cake were topped with chocolate buttercream (see page 29). You could decorate the cake with some truffles around the edge (you would need 10 or 12 for a 20cm (8-inch) size cake).

Special Occasions

Here are suggestions that show you our ideas for assembly and presentation based on the knowledge we have gained from the numerous cupcakes we have made over the past five years for birthdays, anniversaries, events and gatherings. This is where cupcakes come into their own as they can be made and decorated to celebrate virtually any special occasion. You can batch them up to suit your situation, from a few for a child's birthday to several hundred for a large christening or anniversary party. Always be on the look out for imaginative decorations, either in sugar or plastic (but remember to warn guests not to eat the plastic ones!), which can be stored and used when the occasion arises.

Sweetie Cupcakes

Sweetie cupcakes are of course going to attract and delight many a child. Our own children request them over and over again for special occasions, with the added bonus that they can participate in the decorating process.

Makes 12 regular cupcakes

1 batch of Vanilla or Chocolate Cupcakes (see page 15 or 16), regular size
1 batch of Chocolate Buttercream Icing (see page 29)
An assortment of multicoloured sweets, particularly the child's favourites, and/or big soft marshmallows, coloured Smarties, jelly snakes, Maltesers and dolly mixtures

Make up the cupcakes and ice with the chocolate buttercream. You could use vanilla buttercream, but with that one you need to put the sweets on fast before the icing sets, which is why we recommend the chocolate as it takes longer to firm up, giving you more time to decide on which sweets to use and to help if a child is involved in the decorating.

A mixture of different shapes, sizes and colours of sweet will enable you to build them up on top of the icing to create a visual delight. It is always better to use too many than too few and pile them on without hesitation – this is not the recipe to use if worried about sugar content!

FRUIT SALAD £3.40p CORE
TH YOGHURT £ 3· 0p FLOAT £3.50
TH FRUIT AND YOGHURT £3.4 GLASS OF ORGANIC
COLD MILK
£25

Birthday Cupcakes

You could use almost any one of our cupcake flavours to make up a beautiful plate of birthday cupcakes. We have suggested vanilla cupcakes, but of course the birthday girl or boy may have a favourite flavour. You can buy some great packets of sugar lettering from most larger supermarkets to spell out your message, and be as extravagant as you like with decorations and candles. These days it's pretty easy to find an amazing choice of candles in all shapes and sizes to complement the chosen colours and themes of your birthday cupcakes.

Before you start to ice the cupcakes decide on your decorations and message. We would suggest spreading 'Happy Birthday' and the person's name over four regular-size cupcakes or putting one letter per mini cupcake and using as many as you need to spell out your message.

Place the letters on to the cupcakes as soon as you have iced them, trying to keep them in the centre of each cake. Mini cupcakes look really special if you put sprinkles around each letter, then lay out the cupcakes on a large plate or tray to spell out your message. You can do the same if using the lettering on four regular-size cupcakes, reserving any other decorations and some candles for the remaining cupcakes.

Makes 12 regular or
36 mini cupcakes

1 batch of Vanilla Cupcakes (see
    page 15), regular or mini size
1 batch of Vanilla Buttercream
    Icing (see page 26), either in a
    single colour or tinted in a
    variety of shades
1–2 packs of sugar lettering
Candles
Other decorations, such as sugar
    or chocolate sprinkles,
    hundreds and thousands

New Baby Cupcakes

A perfect alternative to a bouquet of flowers for new parents, a box of cupcakes would be greatly appreciated and enjoyed. They are straightforward to put together and can be boxed, ribboned and hand-delivered on your first visit to see the new arrival. You could use one batch of vanilla cupcakes or one batch of lemon cupcakes or half a batch of each.

Make up as many cupcakes as you need to fill your chosen box size. If you are using sugar letters, you can spell out the baby's name on one cupcake or put 'baby boy' or 'baby girl' over a couple of cupcakes and arrange these in the centre of the box.

Then you can decorate the rest of your cupcakes with pinks or blues, or maybe some yellows. Look out for sweet sugar and plastic decorations – ducks, booties, bottles, etc. – in more specialised party shops, or even some sugar baby animals, which can often be found in packets on supermarket shelves. Obviously remind people not to eat the plastic decorations!

Allow the cupcakes to set for 30 minutes or so before boxing so the edges are not too sticky. Carefully arrange your cakes in the box, tape down and tie with ribbon to finish.

1 batch of Vanilla or Lemon Cupcakes (see page 15 or 19), regular size

1 batch of Vanilla Buttercream Icing (see page 26) – we recommend you keep some uncoloured and tint some pale blue or pale pink, depending on the sex of the baby – or Lemon Buttercream Icing (see page 31)

1 pack of sugar lettering (optional) or other appropriate decorations

White cake box

Ribbons

Christening Cupcakes

Christening cupcakes have become extremely popular. Arranged on a tier, they make a stunning centrepiece for a christening buffet. You can choose any flavour of sponge and flavour and colour of buttercream icing. Using our decorating tips and suggestions you can achieve completely professional cupcakes for an intimate gathering or a really large event. Of course, these cupcakes would also be ideal served at a wide variety of celebrations, religious or otherwise – bamitzvahs, naming ceremonies and so on – as they are always well received.

Batches of cupcakes to cater for the number of guests (plus a few to spare), either regular or mini size

Enough buttercream icing for the number of cupcakes you decide on

Packs of sugar lettering in blue or pink

Decorations, such as pale sugar sprinkles, sugared rosebuds, dragees

For a christening we are most often requested to use vanilla or lemon cupcakes (see page 15 or 19) with vanilla or lemon buttercream icing (see page 26 or 31) kept to natural colours or tinted pale shades of baby blue, soft pink or lilac.

Simple decoration is key here – sugared letters in blue or pink used to spell out the baby's name on as many cupcakes as desired or the birth or christening date on others is one idea. Pale sugar sprinkles in white, pearl or pastel shades look sweet, while sugared rosebuds or dainty fresh flowers give a classic, simple and pretty finish.

As an easy alternative you can purchase dragees in many lovely shades from specialist chocolate shops and food halls. Your little cakes will look smart and delicious topped with these. Once they are iced, arrange your cakes on a tier or serving plates.

Anniversary Cupcakes

The versatility of cupcakes means they are ideal for absolutely every anniversary, without exception. As before, it's just a question of deciding on flavours (the favourites of the couple, of course) and cleverly decorating to coincide with the appropriate anniversary. Mini cupcakes work well in party situations as they are the perfect finger food and, what's more, you can serve them with either tea or champagne.

Before you start to ice the cupcakes, decide on your decorations and message. You could spell out the couple's names and/or the date of the anniversary, in sugared letters, placing one letter or number on each cake, or use numbered candles or sparklers purchased from most party shops; you could even arrange the cakes in the shape of the number of years being celebrated.

Once the cupcakes are iced and decorated, serve on pretty silver trays, a large silver cake board or coloured napkins to satisfy the eye and the palate.

As many batches of mini cupcakes as you need for your guests

As many batches of buttercream icing as you need to ice the total number of cupcakes

Decorations to represent the particular anniversary:

- simple silver or gold sugar balls for 25 and 50 years
- edible sugar pearls for 30 years
- sugar and crystallised flowers in appropriate colours
- fresh flowers, such as daffodils (10 years), roses (15 years), lilies (20 years), sweet peas (30 years) and violets (50 years)
- children's plastic rings in the desired colour for a diamond, emerald or ruby anniversary

Packs of sugar lettering

Candles

Weddings

There can be no surprise that a tier of cupcakes has become super-fashionable and increasingly popular for the most prestigious of all cakes, the wedding cake. With so many decisions to make and other people's opinions to deal with during your wedding planning, using cupcakes for the wedding cake makes life really uncomplicated. Quantities can be left until the last minute when the RSVPs are returned and the bride, groom and mothers-in-law can all have their favourite flavour on the day.

A tier of wedding cupcakes can take the form of a traditional classic cake or be totally unconventional: the possibilities are endless. After a few straightforward decisions – flavours of sponge and icings, whether to have a small top cake for cutting, what type of decorations to use – and confirmation of numbers, it's just a matter of simple baking, care and attention with icing and a steady hand in construction.

A tier is still the preferred choice to display the cakes, even for the less traditional of weddings, because height is the best way to create impact. For our very classic orders, more often than not we bake vanilla or almond cupcakes with a complementing vanilla or amaretto buttercream. As decoration, fresh flowers always look beautiful. You could ask the florist creating the bride's bouquet to make a small posy that can rest upon the top cake, but it's just as effective to place the head of a large hydrangea or fragrant garden roses directly on to the top cake, with buds and petals tucked throughout and a few scattered on the table. Keeping the colour scheme consistent and the decoration simple, achieves the effect of one large wedding cake without the tricky cutting, making the whole thing extraordinarily easy for guests to enjoy at the reception or, later, to be individually boxed and presented to guests as they depart.

White Amaretto Cupcakes

These cupcakes are born from the delicious source of sweet almonds that produce the aromatic liqueur amaretto. Feel free to multiply the quantities for however many cupcakes you need for the wedding.

Makes 12 regular cupcakes

110g unsalted butter, at
    room temperature
180g caster sugar
2 large eggs, free-range or organic
125g self-raising flour, sifted
120g plain flour, sifted
125ml semi-skimmed milk, at
    room temperature
½ teaspoon amaretto liqueur or
    almond extract

For the syrup
125g caster sugar
125ml water
½ teaspoon amaretto liqueur or
    almond extract

To decorate
1 batch of Amaretto Buttercream
    Icing (see page 119)
Toasted slivered almonds or other
    decorations or flowers (if the
    flowers have been sprayed or
    are inedible make sure the
    guests know)

Preheat the oven to 160°C (fan)/180°C/350°F/gas mark 4 and line a 12-hole muffin tray with the appropriate size cupcake cases.

In a large mixing bowl cream the butter and sugar until the mixture is pale and smooth, which should take 3–5 minutes using an electric hand mixer. Add the eggs, one at a time, mixing for a few minutes after each addition.

Combine the two flours in a separate bowl. Put the milk in a jug and add the amaretto or almond extract. Add one-third of the flours to the creamed mixture and beat well. Pour in one-third of the milk and beat again. Repeat these steps until all the flour and milk have been added.

Carefully spoon the mixture into the cupcake cases, filling them to about two-thirds full. Bake in the oven for about 25 minutes until slightly raised and golden brown. To check they are cooked, insert a skewer in the centre of one of the cakes – it should come out clean.

Meanwhile, combine the ingredients for the syrup in a microwave-safe bowl and heat until the sugar melts completely (about 1½ minutes); stir to combine. Alternatively heat over a low heat in a saucepan.

Remove the cupcakes from the oven and leave in their tins for about 10 minutes before carefully placing on a wire rack. While they are still warm, dip the tops of the cupcakes into the syrup for a couple of seconds. Return to the wire rack to cool completely.

Ice these cupcakes with amaretto buttercream icing and top with toasted slivered almonds or, for a wedding, use the decorations or fresh flowers chosen by the bride and groom.

Amaretto Buttercream Icing

Perhaps it is the inspired romance brought to the senses by the warm, subtle taste and smell of this icing that makes the amaretto cupcakes a hugely popular choice by impending brides and grooms for the most romantic cake of all! Multiply the recipe according to the number of cupcakes you need to ice.

In a large mixing bowl beat the butter, milk, vanilla extract and half the icing sugar until smooth – this will take a few minutes using an electric hand mixer. Gradually add the remainder of the icing sugar to produce a buttercream of a creamy and smooth consistency.

Add the amaretto or almond extract and beat well. You should taste the icing at this stage as you may wish to add another ¼ teaspoon to make it a little stronger.

The buttercream can be stored in an airtight container for up to 3 days at room temperature. Before re-using, beat well.

Makes enough to ice
15–20 regular cupcakes or
about 60 mini cupcakes

115g unsalted butter, at
   room temperature
60ml semi-skimmed milk, at
   room temperature
1 teapoon good-quality
   vanilla extract
500g icing sugar, sifted
¼ teaspoon amaretto liqueur
   or almond extract (this could
   be increased according to your
   preferred taste)

'Non-traditional' Wedding Cupcakes

For a less traditional affair, many flavours and colours can be mixed. Everything is much less formal: family and friends can help themselves to the flavour they fancy – a choice other cakes cannot offer. And the decorations can definitely be different: how about mini cupcakes topped with old-fashioned loveheart sweets or regular cupcakes adorned with confetti-shaped sprinkles? Simple but effective. There really is no limit to what can be used to represent the bride and groom and the atmosphere they want to create. As an example, we recently delivered a tower of chocolate malted cupcakes in varying sizes, all topped with plastic elephants, and attached to each one was a tiny luggage label with the couple's names handwritten on!

For these less traditional wedding cupcakes on the right, we have used a beautiful silver tier and brightly coloured roses. We once provided wedding cupcakes for a lovely summer wedding in a marquee in the middle of a field, where we set out the cakes on a variety of vintage glass cake plates surrounded by jugs of wild summer flowers.

Before starting, decide on the quantities, flavours and decorations you are going to use. A mix of regular and mini cupcakes is always fun. You could use a complete mixture of flavours of sponge, types of icing and decorations – sprinkles, sugar flowers, sugar hearts, sweets, lettering, figurines and so on.

Bake, ice and decorate the cupcakes and then decide where the tier or plates will be shown at the reception. Place all the cupcakes on the tier as you wish, mixing up the colours and flavours randomly to create a colourful, pretty and delicious display.

'Traditional' Wedding Cupcakes

For this tier of wedding cupcakes we have used a simple Perspex tier, made of flat Perspex plates in varying sizes and interlocking Perspex pieces that create the central spine of the tier. With tiers such as this you can use as many of the levels as you need, depending on the size of the wedding and the number of cakes needed. It is also very unobtrusive and so does not detract from the visual sophistication of the cupcakes.

Make up the number of cupcakes required, either in regular or mini size or a mixture of the two. We would recommend either the amaretto cupcakes (see page 116) or simple vanilla cupcakes (see page 15) with vanilla buttercream (see page 26), left in its natural cream colour. Decide whether you want a top cake for the bride and groom to cut and, if so, what size – the one shown in the picture here is 15cm (6 inches) in size, but an 20cm (8-inch) size would work just as well. The top cake could be made in either chocolate or vanilla sponge and then covered with the same vanilla buttercream you use on the cupcakes.

Make, ice and decorate the top cake first and leave it to sit for a while to allow it to set a little. It is best placed on a silver cake board before icing, which will make it much easier to lift in, to place on the tier and then off again, depending on how much is eaten! Then ice the cupcakes and decorate with the sugar flowers you have chosen. Get the florist to make up a small posy for the top cake and to leave you some spare flowers on the wedding day once they have finished creating the arrangements for the wedding.

Assemble the tier in the exact position where the cakes will be displayed for the wedding reception as it is not advisable to attempt to move it once it has been set up. Carefully place the cupcakes throughout the layers, mixing up the different sizes and not spacing them out too much, as they look much better when they are quite tightly packed. Place the top cake carefully on to the top level. To finish, arrange your posy of flowers in the centre of the top cake. Step back from the display to check it looks okay and then dot some extra flowers or foliage throughout the tier or on the table.

Beyond Cupcakes

Much as we love making cupcakes, there are days when it is still nice to bake a layer cake. In our shops we always have a wide selection of layer cakes available by the slice or to take-away whole. Quite often our customers order a layer cake and some cupcakes, and at other times a simple Victoria sponge or rich chocolate cake fits the bill.

You can bake our selection of layer cakes for a special occasion or for a teatime treat. You can also make the cakes in larger sizes than the 20-cm (8-inch) size we recommend if you have a large number to feed – double the recipe to make two 25 -or 28-cm (10- or 12-inch) layer cakes that can serve 20–25 people easily.

SWEET!
SWEET!

Chocolate Layer Cake

Although slightly more involved than some of our cupcake recipes, this deliciously moist chocolate sponge is well worth the effort. It makes a fantastic birthday or celebration cake, and is always the first choice of all our children.

Makes two 20cm (8-inch) cakes, which can be sandwiched together to make one layer cake

230g good-quality dark chocolate (70% cocoa solids)
170g unsalted butter, at room temperature
350g light soft brown sugar
3 large eggs, free-range or organic, separated
370g plain flour, sifted
1½ teaspoons baking powder
1½ teaspoons bicarbonate of soda
½ teaspoon salt
500ml semi-skimmed milk, at room temperature
2 teaspoons good-quality vanilla extract

To decorate
1 batch of Chocolate or Vanilla Buttercream Icing (see page 26 or 29)
Chocolate sprinkles or other sugar decorations

Preheat the oven to 170°C (fan)/190°C/375°F/gas mark 5. Grease and line two 20cm cake tins with greaseproof paper.

Break the chocolate into pieces and place in a microwave-safe bowl. Melt on a medium setting in 30-second bursts until completely melted. Stir well between each session. Alternatively, place the chocolate in a heatproof bowl over a saucepan of barely simmering water. Stir occasionally until completely melted. Set the bowl aside to cool.

In a large mixing bowl cream the butter and sugar until the mixture is pale and smooth, which should take 3–5 minutes using an electric hand mixer. Put the egg yolks in a separate bowl and beat them for several minutes. Slowly add the egg yolks to the creamed butter and sugar and beat well. Add the cooled chocolate to this mixture and again beat well.

Combine the flour, baking powder, bicarbonate of soda and salt in a separate bowl. Combine the milk and vanilla extract in a jug. Add one-third of the flour to the creamed mixture and beat well. Pour in one-third of the milk and beat again. Repeat these steps until all the flour and milk have been added.

In a clean bowl whisk the egg whites, with clean beaters, until soft peaks start to form. Carefully fold the eggs whites into the main batter using a metal spoon. (Do not beat or you will take all the air out of the mixture.) Divide the mixture evenly between the tins and bake for about 30 minutes. Insert a skewer in the centre of one of the cakes – it should come out clean if it is cooked.

Remove from the oven and leave the cakes in their tins for 10 minutes before turning out on to a wire rack to cool. Peel the greaseproof paper from the bases of the cakes. Once they are cool, sandwich the layers together with vanilla or chocolate buttercream icing and cover the top of the cake with more. Decorate with chocolate sprinkles or other sugar decorations.

The baked sponge layers can be wrapped in clingfilm before icing and will keep at room temperature for up to 3 days or you can freeze them, wrapped, and defrost when needed.

Vanilla Layer Cake

This vanilla layer cake is one of our bakery staples that we are frequently asked for and if you make it in a food processor it takes no time at all. As with most vanilla cake recipes, the list of ingredients is fairly standard, but factor in good-quality ingredients, careful measuring and weighing and setting the correct oven temperatures, and the result is fantastic. We use this as the basis of many a birthday cake, not least because it can be iced and decorated to any effect.

Preheat the oven to 160°C (fan)/180°C/350°F/gas mark 4. Grease and line two 20cm cake tins with greaseproof paper.

Put the butter, sugar, flour, cornflour and baking powder into a food processor. Pulse for a few seconds until evenly mixed. Add the remaining ingredients gradually, processing briefly until just combined. Don't be tempted to overmix or you will take all the air out of the cakes.

If you prefer, you can prepare the mixture with an electric hand mixer. Cream the butter and sugar in a bowl until the mixture is pale and smooth – this should take 3–5 minutes. Combine the dry ingredients in a separate bowl. Add the eggs to the creamed mixture, one at a time, mixing for a few minutes after each addition, alternating with the dry ingredients, and finally the vanilla extract and the milk. Beat well after each addition, but again do not overbeat.

Divide the mixture evenly between the tins and bake in the oven for about 25 minutes until raised and golden brown. Insert a skewer in the centre of one of the cakes – it should come out clean if it is cooked. Remove from the oven and leave the cakes in their tins for about 10 minutes before turning out on to a wire rack to cool. Peel the greaseproof paper from the bases of the cakes.

Once they are cool, sandwich the layers together with half of the buttercream icing and cover the top of the cake with the rest. Decorate the cake with whatever fits with your occasion. As an alternative, for a classic Victoria sponge cake, sandwich the cakes with a thin layer of strawberry or raspberry jam and some vanilla buttercream (uncoloured), or with freshly whipped double cream and some sliced strawberries and dust the top with icing sugar.

Makes two 20cm (8-inch cakes), which can be sandwiched together to make one layer cake

225g unsalted butter, at room temperature
225g caster sugar
210g self-raising flour, sifted
25g cornflour
1 teaspoon baking powder
4 large eggs, free-range or organic
1 teaspoon vanilla extract
3 tablespoons semi-skimmed milk, at room temperature

To decorate – choose one of the following:
- 1 batch of any Buttercream Icing (see pages 26–37)
- 3 tablespoons strawberry or raspberry jam and 1 batch of Vanilla Buttercream Icing (see page 26)
- Whipped cream and fresh strawberries, plus icing sugar, for dusting

Coffee and Walnut Cake

For a most delicious coffee cake, we adapted this inspired sponge from one of Delia Smith's recipes. Combined with our coffee buttercream, it is a coffee-cake connoisseur's delight.

Preheat the oven to 170°C (fan)/190°C/375°F/gas mark 5. Grease and baseline two 20cm cake tins.

In a large mixing bowl cream the butter and sugar until the mixture is pale and smooth, which should take 3–5 minutes using an electric hand mixer. Add the eggs, one at a time, mixing for a few minutes after each addition. Add the flour and baking powder and beat well.

Grind the walnuts in a food processor for about 30 seconds or so – they should not be too fine. Add the coffee and ground walnuts to the batter and mix again but for no more than 3–4 seconds. The mixture should have a marbled effect and it is very important not to overmix or you will take all the air out of the cakes.

Divide the mixture evenly between the tins and bake in the oven for about 25 minutes until raised and golden brown. Insert a skewer in the centre of one of the cakes – it should come out clean if it is cooked.

Remove from the oven and let the cakes cool in their tins. Make up the syrup by combining the ingredients in a jug and stirring well to ensure the sugar dissolves completely. After 10–15 minutes, prick the sponges with a fork, brush on the syrup and leave it to soak in.

When you are ready to ice the cakes, carefully turn them out of their tins and peel the greaseproof paper from the bases. Place one cake on a plate and spread a thin layer of coffee buttercream over it. Place the second cake on top and use the rest of the buttercream to cover the upper surface. Decorate with the walnut halves around the edge.

Makes two 20cm (8-inch) cakes, which can be sandwiched together to make one layer cake

175g unsalted butter, at room temperature
175g golden caster sugar
3 large eggs, free-range or organic
175g self-raising flour, sifted
1½ teaspoons baking powder
75g walnuts
1½ tablespoons instant coffee mixed with 2 tablespoons boiling water

For the syrup
1 tablespoon instant coffee
50g demerara sugar
55ml boiling water

To decorate
1½ batches of Coffee Buttercream Icing (see page 32)
10–12 walnut halves

Lemon Layer Cake

Choose big, juicy lemons and we promise you a deliciously zesty and lively lemon sponge.

Makes two 20cm
(8-inch) cakes, which can
be sandwiched together to
make one layer cake

225g golden caster sugar
225g self-raising flour, sifted
1½ teaspoons baking powder
25g cornflour
225g unsalted butter, at room
    temperature
4 large eggs, free-range or
    organic
Grated zest and juice of
    2 large juicy lemons
    (otherwise
    use 3 lemons)

To decorate
1 batch of Lemon
    Buttercream Icing (see
    page 31)
Sugared lemon slices and/or
    yellow sugar flowers
Grated lemon zest (optional)

Preheat the oven to 170°C (fan)/190°C/375°F/gas mark 5. Grease and baseline two 20cm cake tins.

Put the sugar, flour, baking powder and cornflour in a food processor. Pulse for about 4 seconds until evenly mixed. Add the remaining ingredients and process briefly until evenly blended (roughly 10 seconds). Don't be tempted to overmix.

If you prefer, you can prepare the mixture with an electric hand mixer. Cream the butter and sugar in a bowl until the mixture is pale and smooth. Combine the dry ingredients in a separate bowl. Add the eggs to the creamed mixture, one at a time, mixing for a few minutes after each addition, alternating with the dry ingredients, and finally the grated zest and lemon juice. Beat well after each addition, but again do not overbeat.

Divide the mixture evenly between the tins and bake in the oven for about 25 minutes until raised and golden brown. Insert a skewer in the centre of one of the cakes – it should come out clean if it is cooked. Remove from the oven and leave the cakes in their tins for about 10 minutes before turning out on to a wire rack to cool. Peel the greaseproof paper from the bases of the cakes.

Once they are cool, sandwich the layers together with lemon buttercream icing and cover the top of the cake with more. Decorate with sugared lemon slices or some yellow sugar flowers or both. You could also use some freshly grated lemon zest if you plan to serve the cake immediately, but be aware it will wilt if left too long!

Decorations

Decorating your cupcakes is the time to be at your most imaginative and creative. After the patience and preciseness required to create a perfect sponge and batch of icing, much fun can be had in choosing decorations to complete the picture. You should spend some time thinking about what would be appropriate for the particular cupcakes you are going to make and the occasion they will be eaten at and then tailor your choice of decoration accordingly. You do not need to spend a lot of money on decorations if you are clever with your choices, or need any special skills to decorate, and can make the finished product as simple or as complicated and extravagant as you want.

Almost anything can be used as a cake decoration. It certainly does not always need to be edible, as plastic figurines or fresh flowers can be equally pretty (just don't let anyone try to eat them!). In the last five years it has become much easier to buy a huge selection of sugar cake decorations. Most larger supermarkets and party shops now stock sugar sprinkles in a variety of colours, packets of sugar animals and sugar flowers, crystallised rose and violet petals, gold and silver sugar balls, chocolate curls, coffee beans, chocolate and liqueur truffles, candles, plastic cake toppers and figurines, and other decorations that can be sought out through the aisles.

As shown in our recipe for sweetie cupcakes (see page 102) you can use any variety of sweet or chocolate to decorate your cupcakes, all of which can be bought from the local newsagent confectioner or a bespoke chocolate shop. For the cupcakes made using fresh fruits, you can use the grated zest of oranges, lemons or limes to decorate, or whole strawberries or raspberries.

One of the advantages of using buttercream icing on cupcakes is that it is much easier to decorate, as it never sets completely hard and gives a much better and deeper surface with which to experiment. If you are unhappy with what you have done, you can simply remove the decorations and start again. Equally, if you feel you are not particularly good at icing, you can easily use decorations to cover up any mistakes – simply use a few more sprinkles and no one will ever know.

If you are making cupcakes with children, it is a good idea to let them be in charge of the decorating at the end. Allow them to throw on whatever they have chosen – although it's probably safer to use smaller sugar sprinkles if the children are small – and it will fill an enjoyable afternoon and create a colourful and delicious treat.

At the other end of the scale, if decorating your own or somebody else's wedding cupcakes, take extra care when choosing the decorations and make sure you have bought them some time in advance (unless using fresh flowers of course) so there is no disappointment on the day.

However, whatever kind of decorations you decide on, just remember to have fun with them and look around for the most interesting and original ones you can find. It is a very personal choice and different people like completely different things, so you should always go with your instincts and be sure it will work out brilliantly. We have found choosing the decorations for our cupcakes one of the most enjoyable things we do and still feel delight when we chance upon something new.

Techniques

We want to share the techniques we have found to be most useful in achieving success with our Primrose Bakery cupcakes and layer cakes.

• Sourcing the best quality ingredients at your disposal and budget will make a big difference to the end result. These include free-range or organic eggs, whole or semi-skimmed milk and a good-quality unsalted dairy butter. If organic is your first choice, you will find that organic icing sugar will not produce the creamy buttercreams we make. It is unfortunately grainy and, in its natural state, discoloured, making it impossible to produce the pretty pastels we prefer to use.

• Correct storage is paramount with storecupboard ingredients to ensure longevity and freshness. Remember to check use-by dates, especially on ingredients not regularly used and on spices and essences which remain on the shelf because of the small quantities needed at any one time. Airtight containers with lock-on lids are the best way of keeping dry ingredients as well as storing finished cupcakes overnight. If you choose to freeze uniced cupcakes, do this when they are completely cool. Never be tempted to store iced cupcakes in the fridge as this will spoil their freshness of flavour and texture. If baking in the summer, ice at the last possible moment and keep in the coolest shade available.

• Before starting to bake, it is best to bring all ingredients to room temperature. Butter should be soft but not melted: by leaving out the correct quantity for an hour or so before baking you should have the perfect consistency. Make sure the oven is at the correct temperature before putting the cakes in and always try not to open the oven door while they are baking.

• Careful measuring of ingredients can make a huge difference too, so don't be tempted to guess at quantities too much or add in something extra on a whim! Good electric weighing scales are fantastic and will measure wet and dry ingredients.

• It is most important to have plenty of time and patience when baking and really enjoy what you are doing – that way your cakes will turn out brilliantly and can be enjoyed by all, including yourself.

Utensils/Equipment

You certainly do not need every piece of equipment on this list to bake perfect cupcakes – it is more a suggestion of some of the things we think you will find useful for baking of all kinds. We do feel an electric hand mixer is very useful, making the process easier and quicker. They are relatively cheap and easy to find in the shops or online.

Good scales, preferably electric

Large mixing bowls

Measuring spoons

Measuring jug

Electric hand mixer

Food processor

Sieve

Grater

Muffin trays (regular and mini size)

Cupcake cases (regular and mini size)

Spatulas

Wooden spoons

Cake testers – a skewer will do

Wire cooling racks

Greaseproof paper

Clingfilm

20cm (8-inch) cake tins with removable bottoms or
    springform

Palette knives or flat unserrated knives for icing

Airtight containers

Oven timer

Baking sheets

Index

Stockists

Primrose Bakery
www.primrosebakery.org.uk
Cafe, cupcakes to order, candles, toys, cards, tableware
Primrose Hill: 69 Gloucester Avenue, London NW1 8LD
Tel: 020 7483 4222
Covent Garden: 42 Tavistock Street, London WC2E 7PB
Tel: 020 7836 3638
Email: primrose-bakery@btconnect.com

John Lewis
www.johnlewis.com
Bakeware, equipment
Branches nationwide
Mail order 08456 049049

Waitrose
www.waitrose.com
Ingredients, decorations,
cupcake cases
Branches nationwide, home delivery

Sainsbury's
www.sainsburys.co.uk
Ingredients, decorations,
cupcake cases
Branches nationwide, home delivery

Marks and Spencer
www.marksandspencer.com
Ingredients, decorations,
cupcake cases
Branches nationwide

Fortnum and Mason
www.fortnumandmason.com
Jams, chocolates and sweets for use as
decorations, specialist ingredients
0845 300 1707
Mail order
181 Piccadilly, London W1A 1ER

Divertimenti
www.divertimenti.co.uk
0870 1295026
Mail order, 2 shops in London, 1
shop in Cambridge
Bakeware, equipment, display plates,
specialist ingredients, cupcake cases

www.cakecraftshop.co.uk
01732 464826
Equipment, bakeware, packaging,
boxes, cake boards, decorations,
wedding tiers, icing colours
Mail order

Rococo chocolates
www.rococochocolates.com
0208 761 8456
Mail order, 3 shops in London

Jane Asher cake shop
www.jane-asher.co.uk
0207 584 6177
Equipment, packaging, decorations,
candles, cupcake cases
Mail order, 1 shop in London

Selfridges food hall
www.selfridges.com
4 stores nationwide
0800 123 400
Specialist ingredients, especially ones
from the USA

Lakeland
www.lakeland.co.uk
015394 88100
Mail order, shops nationwide
Equipment, bakeware, packaging,
cupcake cases, decorations

Harvey Nichols food hall
www.harveynichols.com
7 stores nationwide
Specialist ingredients, especially from
abroad and USA